UNITE History
Volume 4 (1960–1974)

The Transport and General Workers' Union (TGWU):
The Great Tradition of Independent Working-Class Power

UNITE History
Volume 4
(1960–1974)

The Transport and
General Workers' Union (TGWU):
The Great Tradition of Independent
Working-Class Power

John Foster

LIVERPOOL UNIVERSITY PRESS

First published 2022 by
Liverpool University Press
4 Cambridge Street
Liverpool
L69 7ZU

British Library Cataloguing-in-Publication data
A British Library CIP record is available

ISBN 978-1-80207-703-2

Typeset by Carnegie Book Production, Lancaster
Printed and bound by CPI Group (UK) Ltd, Croydon CR0 4YY

Contents

Figures

Boxes

Acknowledgements

Many people have assisted in the writing of this volume. Those active trade unionists of the 1960s and 1970s, who themselves helped to make this history, generously shared their memories. Their contributions are acknowledged throughout the text. Of those who helped write this volume, tribute must be paid first of all to the late Graham Stevenson. Graham conceived the idea of the history, was himself a leading officer of the Transport and General Workers Union (TGWU), and wrote the section on racism and the fight against it. His death was a major loss to the working-class movement.

Professor Mary Davis has contributed the section on the fight for women's rights and equality, Alex Klemm on equal pay in Ireland and Dr John Fisher, previous director of research and education for the union, the section on containerisation in the Southampton docks.

The regional teams contributed greatly and helped overcome problems of access to archives posed by the Covid pandemic through 2020 and 2021. Particular thanks should go to Donal O'Cofaigh and the staff of the Unite office in Belfast and to the late Mel Corry and Dr Sean Byers of Trademark. Ann Field in London opened the way for interviews with key figures in the print industry.

The review panel for the TGWU history provided invaluable comments on the manuscript, helping to eliminate many errors and clarify key issues: Dr Ken Fuller, Chris Kaufman, Professor Roger Seifert, Dr Tom Sibley and, not least, Professor Chris Wrigley. So also did colleagues on the TGWU writing team including Professor Marjorie Mayo and Adrian Weir, former assistant chief of staff, Unite.

Abbreviations

ACTSS	Association of Clerical, Technical and Supervisory Staff
AEF	Amalgamated Union of Engineering and Foundry Workers
AEI	Amalgamated Electrical Industries
AESD	Association of Engineering and Shipbuilding Draughtsmen
AEU	Amalgamated Engineering Union
ASLEF	Associated Society of Locomotive Engineers and Firemen
ASTMS	Association of Scientific, Technical and Managerial Staffs
ATGWU	Amalgamated Transport and General Workers Union
AUEW	Amalgamated Union of Engineering Workers
BALPA	British Airline Pilots Association
BAT	British American Tobacco
BICC	British Insulated Calender's Cables
BL	British Library
BMC	British Motor Corporation
BOAC	British Overseas Airways Corporation
BRS	British Road Services
BTDB	British Transport Docks Board
CBI	Confederation of British Industry
CND	Campaign for Nuclear Disarmament
COBRA	Cabinet Office Briefing Room A
DATA	Draughtsmen and Allied Technicians Association
DEA	Department of Economic Affairs
DPR	Democratic People's Republic
EEC	European Economic Community
ETU	Electrical Trades Union
FUE	Federated Union of Employers
FWUI	Federated Workers Union of Ireland
GDR	German Democratic Republic
GEC	General Electric Company
GLA	Greater London Authority
ICFTU	International Confederation of Free Trade Unions

ICI	Imperial Chemical Industries
ICTU	Irish Congress of Trade Unions
ILP	Independent Labour Party
IMF	International Monetary Fund
ITGWU	Irish Transport and General Workers Union
JSSC	Joint Shop Stewards Committee
LCDTU	Liaison Committee for the Defence of Trade Unions
MP	Member of parliament
NATO	North Atlantic Treaty Organization
NATSOPA	National Association of Operative Printers and Assistants
NDLB	National Dock Labour Board
NEC	National Executive Committee
NEDC	National Economic Development Council
NGA	National Graphical Association
NI	Northern Ireland
NIC	Northern Ireland Committee
NICRA	Northern Ireland Civil Rights Association
NJACCWER	National Joint Action Campaign Committee for Women's Equal Rights
NUGMW	National Union of General and Municipal Workers
NUM	National Union of Mineworkers
NUR	National Union of Railwaymen
NUVB	National Union of Vehicle Builders
NWA	National Wage Agreements
OPEC	Organisation of Petroleum Exporting Countries
PIB	Prices and Incomes Board
RUC	Royal Ulster Constabulary
SCM	Scottish Commercial Motormen
SLADE	Society of Lithographic Artists, Designers and Engravers
SOGAT	Society of Graphical and Allied Trades
STUC	Scottish Trade Union Congress
T&G	Abbreviation for TGWU
TASS	Technical Administrative and Supervisory Section
TGWU	Transport and General Workers Union
TUC	Trades Union Congress
UCS	Upper Clyde Shipbuilders
UDLA	Ulster Democratic Labour Association
UUP	Ulster Unionist Party
UVF	Ulster Volunteer Force
WFTU	World Federation of Trade Unions

Foreword

Unite History Project
The Six-Volume History

2022 marks the centenary of the formation of the Transport & General Workers' Union (T&G), now a part of Unite, Britain and Ireland's largest union in private industry. The T&G was also a significant workers' organisation in public-sector employment, a tradition carried forward into Unite.

The T&G was the first general trade union, taking pride in organising workers in every occupation and delivering collective bargaining across a multitude of industries. The T&G held real industrial power through much of its history, and it was from this basis that millions of working people won better pay and conditions that dramatically improved living standards.

The union also exercised a great deal of political influence, particularly within the Labour Party. This and its interaction with government, often as a powerful independent actor in its own right, provide the setting for a wider chronological history of the labour movement in Britain – and to that extent also the industrial and political history of Britain; it was not without a significant impact in Ireland as well.

This history reflects and exposes the wider processes of social change in which working people played an active role, in terms of creating an understanding of oppression in society and exploitation, particularly of women and black people, in the workplace. In addition, the union's international work and campaigns are brought into sharp focus.

Many of the T&G's general secretaries, from Bevin to Morris, have been the subject of biographies, and Jack Jones published an autobiography. But this series is different: among other things it examines how the union's central function, campaigning and winning on jobs, pay and conditions, evolved over the course of the twentieth century.

This six-volume series tells this story in a highly original way, as it enables the incorporation of local history as played out by the union's shop stewards and branch officers. Work has been undertaken at regional level, based on interviews and newly uncovered archival material, that brings our history to life and gives a human dimension to an otherwise 'top level' narrative. Unions are after all composed of individuals – in the T&G's case, hundreds of thousands.

I believe that these volumes will make a great contribution to Unite's educational programmes with its members, workplace representatives and other activists, and more generally in colleges and universities; nothing like this work has been published before.

If we are to avoid the mistakes of the past it is of course essential that we understand and learn from it! This series of six books, detailing the history of one of the twentieth century's most important and vital trade unions, gives us that opportunity, and I commend them to you.

Sharon Graham
General Secretary
Unite the Union

'The Great Tradition of Independent Working-Class Power'
Jack Jones, 1967

Introduction

*The Labour Party must turn its energies into making conscious
socialists of the many millions of trade union members and
co-operators who, by their allegiance to the Labour Movement, are
already socialists in embryo.*[1]

This was Frank Cousins's response to the attempt by the Labour leader
Hugh Gaitskell to delete the socialist Clause 4 from the Labour Party
constitution. It was also his answer to the claims made at the time that
workers were no longer interested in socialism. The intervention by the
Transport and General Workers Union (TGWU) was critical in rallying
support from other trade unions to ensure Gaitskell's defeat in the Labour
Party's executive and preserving the party's socialist objectives. In the
same year, 1960, the TGWU also narrowly succeeded in reversing Labour
support for nuclear weapons.

These interventions marked the beginnings of a transformation of
both the British trade union movement and of British politics more widely.
This volume tells the story of how it was achieved and what the TGWU
contributed. It focuses in particular on the processes by which the union's
members themselves became a key driving force for progressive social
change, many of them becoming, as Cousins put it, 'conscious socialists'.
Initially the advance was tentative and halting and dependent on a few
determined individuals. The opposition to nuclear weapons was soon
reversed and, although Clause 4 remained, successive Labour leaders,
Gaitskell and then Wilson, happily ignored it. Yet within a decade, the
TGWU was at the heart of a trade union alliance that first stopped a
Labour government introducing anti-trade union laws and then defeated

---

1 TGWU *Record*, January 1960, p.28.

a much more determined Conservative government. By then, in the early 1970s, this transformation had assumed a mass character. The working-class movement redeveloped a level of class solidarity not seen since the 1920s exemplifying, as Jack Jones put it in 1967, the 'great tradition of independent working-class power'.

This volume seeks to explain how this was achieved. Initially it did largely depend on individuals, among whom the two successive TGWU general secretaries, Frank Cousins and Jack Jones, played a critical role. Soon, however, it became a collective endeavour. Workplaces and their wider communities drove the change. Longbridge, London's Royal Docks, Dagenham, Clydeside's shipyards, Merseyside's giant factories and docks, Fleet Street print and the giant international airport at Heathrow became the fortresses of this new movement. The voices of the women and men who collectively built these fortresses can still be heard.

Section I will look at the early stages of this transformation in the years to 1966. It will seek to understand the material circumstances that triggered this change, for change did not result simply from the convictions of individuals. These were the years that saw the creation of a new nationwide shop stewards movement, the organisation of one-day strikes across the engineering industry and the time when the principle of all-union shops was increasingly defended by strike action. This happened not by chance but in a period of intense industrial transformation. Government and big business sought to see off international competition through the creation of giant companies and to reduce wage costs by moving production into low-wage regions. Macmillan's Conservative government, and then Labour under Harold Wilson, looked to draw the Trades Union Congress (TUC) and union leaderships into a partnership that endorsed such corporate-led planning and to hold wages in check.

The TGWU under Cousins resisted. Planning and investment was one thing. Doing so at workers' expense was another. Cousins sought to create a counter alliance with the TUC and the Labour Left and later, while a member of the 1964 Labour government, to argue for socialist planning. His efforts were blocked.

At the same time workers in industry resisted the infringements of wages and conditions. These years saw plant-level bargaining, led by shop stewards, becoming the norm. Managements sought to intensify work under the guise of productivity bargaining. Workers resisted by exercising their local power and united across combines to prevent the exploitation of regional differentials. Strike action, much of it local and 'unofficial', reached new heights. All of it involved sacrifice and often loss of employment. Some of it brought active solidarity from workers in other plants and other trades. Sometimes, however, the battles to defend existing differentials and maintain sectional control of work became (at least implicitly) discriminatory – re-enforcing differentials and exclusions against women and ethnic minorities. During these early years, during the first half of the 1960s, the ultimate political direction remained unclear.

Section II examines the role of the TGWU under the second Wilson government between 1966 and 1970. Here the battle lines were more clearly drawn. Cousins made clear his belief that Labour's alliance with corporate capitalism, whatever the level of union involvement, would never lead to socialism. Equally, any attempt to legally shackle shop stewards at plant level would immobilise precisely those forces that were needed to secure socialist change. In this belief he was joined by Jack Jones, who took over as general secretary in 1969, and by Hugh Scanlon, newly elected leader of the engineers. But it was those in Britain's factories and workplaces who actually resisted and stalled the Labour government's attempt to enforce statutory restrictions on wages. At the same time it was the newly formed Liaison Committee for the Defence of Trade Unions (LCDTU) that provided the national organisation needed to unite both shop steward combines and local union committees against the subsequent legislative attack on trade union rights.

The Labour government's failure to honour its socialist promises combined with its direct attack on the rights of organised labour had contradictory consequences politically. In some areas it led to demoralisation and opened the way for the populist right. Enoch Powell sought to build an anti-immigration movement and in 1968 a (very) small section of the London dockers struck work in his support. In the Midlands these years also saw issues of race dividing some workforces. Nationally Cousins led the TGWU in a campaign against all forms of racism. The intensifying level of wage struggles also highlighted the degree to which existing workplace differentials embedded gender discrimination and thereby split the workforce. The 1968 strike by women machinists from Ford at both Dagenham and Halewood marked a key milestone. Thereafter, the battle for the principle of equal pay for equal work became a far more general objective within the trade union movement.

Overall, however, the later 1960s saw the beginnings of a key turning point in attitudes and ideas. Joint shop stewards committees (JSSCs) brought a new unity between different trades and grades and began to assert sharply different perspectives from those of corporate shareholders about the social character and purpose of production and investment. In this they were actively encouraged by Cousins and Jones within the TGWU. When in 1969 the Labour government finally announced legislation to impose penal sanctions on individual strikers it was met for the first time since 1926 by one-day political general strikes. The scale of these strikes put backbone into an otherwise malleable TUC. The Labour government backed down.

The volume's final section looks at the culmination of the process of radicalisation under Edward Heath's Conservative government. Heath sought to co-opt trade union leaders by making them and their unions legally responsible for the actions of their members. It also sought to do so in new conditions in which unemployment was allowed to rise to near a million and financial support was withdrawn from economically marginal workplaces. Initially this set back resistance. But within a year it had had a quite contrary effect. Much broader issues were raised as threatened workplaces struggled against closure – issues that galvanised surrounding communities and industrial regions around the slogan of the 'right to work'. Over 100 workplace occupations followed the work-in at Upper Clyde Shipbuilders (UCS) in July 1971. February 1972 saw mass pickets from Birmingham car industry blockading the Saltley Gate coke depot in a solidarity action with the striking miners. That summer, when the government sought to enforce the new law against the London dockers, the call for a General Strike from the LCDTU brought out workers in their millions. The fortresses of the working class held firm. The government capitulated.

In the course of these struggles a new young generation of 'conscious socialists' was created that would fight on for the principles of working-class solidarity and socialism through the difficult years of the 1980s and 1990s. This volume seeks to tell their story – as far as possible using their own words.

I

1960–1966

The first chapter documents the rise of the shop stewards' movement through the early 1960s and the second chapter on the TGWU's defence of the Labour Party's socialist principles from 1960 onwards. The third looks at the relations between Frank Cousins, the TGWU and the first Wilson government. Each chapter will begin by examining the role of a particular workplace or industry in this process: Longbridge, Heathrow Airport and the London docks.

1

'Making Working People Bear the Burden'[1]

How the Macmillan's Conservative government sought to reverse industrial decline by boosting the corporate profit share – but instead created a mass shop stewards movement

Longbridge: A Fortress of the Working-class Movement

By the 1960s the British Motor Corporation (BMC)'s Longbridge plant, based on a 30-acre site west of Birmingham, had a workforce of over 12,000. Established in 1905 by Herbert Austin, it became the core plant for Austin Motors. By the 1920s Austin had become one of the three big motor manufacturers operating in Britain. At that point Austin, along with Morris and the US company Ford, produced up to two thirds of national car output. Forty years later Longbridge had become the heart of the BMC, the giant company resulting from the merger of the two big British firms, Austin and Morris, in 1952.

Before 1940 the Longbridge factory had been largely non-union. During the war union membership increased but still covered only a minority of the workforce. The turning point for unionisation came in 1956 when the management sought to re-assert detailed workplace control by exploiting the Suez crisis credit squeeze to dismiss 2,000 workers. A strong intervention by the TGWU, led by regional officer Jack Jones, gave official support to a strike called by the conveners. Four weeks of mass picketing, backed by solidarity action from London and Liverpool dockers, led to re-instatement and an agreement on work-sharing. Subsequently almost all workers joined a union.

1 Jack Jones, 1961.

In 1960 there were 245 officially recognised shop stewards at Longbridge. Of these, 90 were TGWU, 169 from the engineers' union Amalgamated Engineering Union (AEU) and 96 from the National Union of Vehicle Builders. They were united in a works committee convened by Dick Etheridge. The chair was from the TGWU, the treasurer from the Electrical Trades Union (ETU) and minute secretary from the Sheet Metal Workers Union. The Committee also included a member from the Vehicle Builders. The convener Dick Etheridge, an AEU member, dealt daily with disputes as they arose on the shop floor: holiday pay; work allocation; compensation for lost time as a result of disputes elsewhere in the supply chain; new working practices. Almost always they involved members of all unions. In many cases, where management failed to respond, they warranted notification to the Confederation of Shipbuilding and Engineering Unions (the 'Confed') of a management 'failure to agree'. As convener, Etheridge also had to ensure all workers were informed of wider developments. On 15 September 1960 there was a delegate meeting for all Birmingham car workers to discuss the opening of car factories in Scotland, North West England and South Wales and the urgent 'need for an interchange of information'. There were regular appeals for solidarity and financial assistance from workplaces elsewhere, e.g. from the Handley Page Joint Strike Committee for support of their strike against the dismissal of their works convener and the appeal from the JSSC of International Harvester, Doncaster, in a dispute over union recognition.[2]

Longbridge remained at the forefront of wage militancy throughout the decade. In 1969 its workers struck work in the one-day protest against the Labour government's proposed legislation to criminalise unofficial strikes, the first coordinated national strike action on a political issue since 1926. In 1972 it sent one of the largest contingents to support the miners at Saltley Gate.

Kevin Halpin, then chair of the LCDTU, recalls the impact when the factory contingents marched in:

> That morning the police were cock-a-hoop as their numbers had again cleared the miners from the plant gates and allowed coal trucks to sweep through. Then they turned and [...] saw on the crest of the hill a banner and swelling beneath it a vast body of people who flooded irresistibly down the slope to join the miners and occupy the road in solidarity. The police could do nothing: they simply retired, overwhelmed. The defeat of the Midlands

2 Modern Records Centre (hereafter MRC) MSS 202/5A/3/1/22, Papers of Dick Etheridge, Annual meeting of AEU shop stewards; 202/A/3/1/23 and 24, shop steward correspondence 1960 and 1961.

Figure 1: Pickets at Saltley Gate coke depot 1972
(Image: Tony Coult)

Constabulary, reckoned at 1,000 strong, by tens of thousands of workers was historic.[3]

By 1974 Longbridge was seen, by both friend and foe, as one of the great fortresses of the British working class.

The Rise of a New Shop Stewards Movement

The 1960s and 1970s witnessed the power of the shop stewards movement at its peak. These years saw shop-floor workers gaining in confidence and assertiveness, and increasingly questioning both management authority and corporate judgement. They also presented a growing challenge to government as, first, the Conservatives and then Labour sought to impose various forms of wage restraint. By the early 1970s, there was also an

---

3 Kevin Halpin, *Memoirs of a Militant* (Praxis Press, 2012), p.117.

increasing level of unity between different grades, skills and unions at shop-floor level.

The heart of this transformation was in the new mass production consumer durable industries that had developed in the Midlands and South East in the interwar period. Post-war they expanded further and became the basis of Britain's export drive: electrical goods, cars, motorcycles, refrigerators, office equipment. It was in these industries that the TGWU, particularly as a result of its merger with the Workers Union, had built a base in the 1930s among the 'non-skilled' production workers who staffed the assembly lines.

Traditionally the TGWU had a highly centralised structure of wage bargaining. Formed during the mass unemployment of post-1921 deflation, the union had been stabilised by the deals negotiated by Ernest Bevin with major employers in transport, docks and consumer goods. The union received recognition in return for long-term wage settlements and in some cases, especially after 1926, this also involved explicit agreements on the avoidance of strikes. To police these arrangements the union employed an army of full-time officers. Sometimes these full-time officers – as Jack Jones noted in Liverpool – became far too close to the employers. Others, however, as both Frank Cousins and Jack Jones themselves demonstrated, became the mainstays of union recruitment through a combative assertion of workers' rights. But in both cases, through the unemployment of the 1930s, the union's survival and growth depended as much on its full-time staff as on shop stewards in the workplace or its lay branch officers.[4]

In the wartime and then during post-war full employment, this balance was reversed. Shop stewards increasingly led action on wages and day-to-day bargaining. There were two causes. One was inflation: the steady year-by-year rise in consumer prices. The other was the opportunity for redress within the workplace of past injustices. The new wage systems that accompanied assembly-line mass production enabled stewards to take charge of local bargaining. Over the previous four decades wage rates across engineering, and manufacturing in general, had been set through national level bargaining between unions, mainly representing skilled workers, and the national employers' federation, a pattern reasserted after the 1922 engineering lockout. Employers, especially medium-sized and smaller employers, wanted a national system that could re-enforce their local authority and take wage bargaining out of the workplace. Under these national agreements wage levels were negotiated within two rigid bands: skilled workers and labourers.

4 Kevin Whitson traces these developments both before and after the Second World War in 'Politics of Production in the Engineering Industry', *Labour History Review*, 2016, vol.81, no.1, pp.1–24 and in 'The Origins of Disorderly Wage Bargaining in the British Engineering Industry', *Historical Studies in Industrial Relations* (hereafter *HSIR*), 2010, vol. 29/30, pp.33–60.

Increasingly, however, this did not suit the bigger employers, especially those bringing in new technologies and production methods from the United States and using piecework payment and time and motion to maximise output from the new assembly lines. These employers wanted more detailed control over the production process and were willing buy off workers at plant level to do so. In the 1930s when unemployment was high, these innovations had limited wider impact. However, the rearmament drive from 1939 and then post-war full employment gave shop-floor workers a new bargaining power. In the fight to maintain real wages they were able to exploit these new management techniques and in the course of doing so eroded long-established differentials. This in turn provoked a revolt by sections of the skilled engineering work force. One result was the Coventry Toolroom Agreement of 1941 negotiated by Bevin as wartime Minister of Labour. This guaranteed that the wages of the highly skilled tool-setters would rise in line with the rates achieved by non-skilled assembly workers – a tacit recognition that control over wages had effectively passed to shop-floor bargaining.[5]

This pattern was maintained after the war. Inflation continued. Plant-level productivity bargaining also increased, particularly as a result of new US plants moving to Britain in the late 1940s and 1950s to penetrate European markets and utilise cheaper British labour. US firms wanted if possible to exclude trade union recognition and bargain wages outside the existing collective bargaining structures operated at national level by British engineering employers.[6] They also saw direct workplace productivity bargaining as giving them greater control over the production process. However, this did not always work in their favour. TGWU itself negotiated one of the most celebrated of these productivity agreements at Esso's Fawley refinery in Southampton in 1960, which provided many opportunities for subsequent amendment in favour of the workers.[7] In

---

5 Richard Croucher, 'The Coventry Toolroom Agreement, 1941–1972, Part 1: Origins and Operation', *HSIR*, 1999, vol.8, no.1, pp.1–41; Croucher, 'The Coventry Toolroom Agreement, 1941–1972, Part 2: Abolition', *HSIR*, 2000, vol.9, no. 1, pp.37–70.

6 Bill Knox and Alan McKinlay, 'Working for the Yankee Dollar: American Inward Investment and Scottish Labour, 1945-70', *HSIR*, 1999, vol.7, no.1, pp.1–26.

7 This agreement became famous not so much because it broke new ground but because Allan Flander's *The Fawley Productivity Agreements: A Case Study of Management and Collective Bargaining* (Faber, 1964) was effectively a manifesto for a new collaborative system of industrial relations. Flanders himself was a leading figure on the Gaitskellite right wing of the Labour Party running the US-state department financed *Socialist Commentary* jointly with Rita Hinden. Bruce Ahlstrand, *The Quest for Productivity: A Case Study of Fawley After Flanders* (Cambridge University Press, 1990) details this political background and exposes both Flander's misleading estimates of productivity and the degree to which shop stewards were subsequently able to turn the agreement in the interests of the workforce.

all cases such agreements made shop-floor representation of even greater importance to defend the wage levels. Each production process in each workplace was now a focus of negotiation. Work stoppages on the production line became a key tool. In doing so each group of workers developed their own cohesion and leadership and created a new pattern of industrial relations distinguished by a far more combative and mobilised workforce.

However, there were some adverse aspects. Les Kealey, writing in the TGWU *Record* for July 1961, highlighted some of them. He noted that basic wage rates themselves were 'unjustifiably low'. Actual earnings, on the other hand, were often much higher and 'made up of various systems of increments additional to basic rates'.[8] This, he suggested, was discriminatory because it did not apply to all workers. Those in areas where there was more limited bargaining leverage remained on the basic labourer's rate. He therefore urged a radical increase in basic rates that also reduced differentials.

The new bargaining structures did therefore hold the potential for division, sectionalism and discrimination. As management constantly reorganised production, demarcation became a major issue. Black and ethnic minority workers tended to be relegated to labouring jobs with little leverage (a significant minority of those from the Indian subcontinent actually had university degrees but few had relevant apprenticeship training in engineering). And still more centrally there was the position of women. By 1960 women made up a third of the full-time labour force. But, as Geoffrey Goodman noted in *The Record* for March 1961, although the principle of equal pay for equal work had been conceded in the public sector, this was definitely not the case elsewhere: 'employers in private industry have always fiercely resisted equal pay as they did shorter hours'. He urged the union to tackle 'progressive employers first' in a new campaign for equality.[9]

Significant dangers did therefore exist. We will see later that a number of disputes did arise in which ethnicity was a key factor of division. The battle for equal pay was also one in which the social acceptance of existing injustice blocked advance. The 1961 TGWU biennial conference unanimously passed a motion demanding equal pay for equal work noting that similar motions had been passed before without notable effect and hence greater attention had to be given to organisation. As Eileen McCulloch, the TGWU's National Women's Officer stressed in the *Record* in February 1961, it would have to be women who took the initiative.[10]

8 TGWU *Record*, July 1961.
9 TGWU *Record*, March 1961.
10 MRC MSS 126/TG/1887/19, 1961 Biennial Conference, minute 26; TGWU *Record*, February 1961.

Nonetheless, overall the trend of the 1960s was not towards sectionalism and division. It was in the other direction. Solidarity action with other workers increased, as did the defence of the principles of collective bargaining, 100 per cent trade union membership and a broader agenda of political change. To understand why, we have to look beyond economic factors to the way people argued and mobilised in the workplace and how it enabled the Left to develop its influence.

The Left in the TGWU

As previous volumes have demonstrated, the TGWU incorporated and carried forward at least some of the radicalism that had mobilised Britain's working-class movement during and immediately after the First World War. Its two key components were originally workers in the docks and passenger transport. In both sectors the Left had been strongly organised and remained for a time dominant. Despite Bevin's drive to exert centralised and increasingly right-wing control, Left influence was never entirely displaced and from the 1930s it was to some extent strengthened in some localities by the adhesion of the Workers Union, founded on syndicalist principles by Tom Mann in 1912, and still including militants defending the principles of workplace power. In the 1960s the TGWU's leadership itself represented the continuity of this tradition. Throughout his union career Frank Cousin had waged a long battle against bureaucratic centralism and was closely aligned to the left wing of the Labour Party. Jack Jones was also deeply immersed in the culture of the Left and had himself fought in the Spanish Civil War.

The Left as it existed in the 1960s is probably best defined by a commitment to socialism in the terms defended by Frank Cousins: that is, the social ownership of the means of production, distribution and exchange. It would generally include an understanding that any such transformation would require the political use of the *collective* strength of working people as a class – a position originally held by Bevin himself prior to 1926. It did not necessarily involve an endorsement of socialism as developed in the USSR but it did involve an openness to study its achievements, as Cousins himself did, and an opposition to the politics of the Cold War and of British colonialism.

Motions to the 1961 biennial conference in support of Clause 4 show where this Left was then concentrated. By far the largest number of 'Left' motions came from London and East Region – from 61 branches in all. Next came the Midlands with 32, South West with 20 and Yorkshire and Humberside and the North East with ten each. Relatively few at that stage came from Scotland (eight), North West (six), Wales (five), Merseyside (three) – regions where the new industries had as yet made limited impact and where full-timers appointed by Arthur Deakin, Bevin's right-wing successor, were often still entrenched.[11] Cousins himself intervened against right-wing officials on Merseyside in February 1961 when they sought to dismiss shop stewards who had called a strike against freezing conditions in the Dunlop rubber factory.[12] In London Jack Dash describes the officials overseeing the docks as carrying forward the worst attitudes of the Deakin era.[13]

This new developing Left was drawn from a variety of backgrounds ranging from the Independent Labour Party (ILP), supporters of Aneurin Bevan and the pre-war Socialist League to the Communist Party. It often tended to be left-wingers who took on the role of shop stewards, always a challenging job and one that often invited retaliation and victimisation. It also tended to be those on the Left who were elected to the even more difficult and demanding roles of workplace convener. If we think of the workplace fortresses emerging in this period, it was in Birmingham Dick Etheridge in Longbridge, Peter Nicholas at Rover and Arthur Harper at Leyland Tractors. On Clydeside it was George McCormack at Rolls Royce Hillington, George Grant at Babcocks, Jim Airlie at Govan Yard and Sam Barr at Scotstoun (though also note the presence of Gavin Laird sustained by Catholic Action at Singer in Clydebank). On Merseyside it was Stan Pemberton at Dunlop and Bobby Owens at British Leyland (both Left Labour). At Dagenham it was Sid Harroway and in the London docks, at least unofficially, Jack Dash. In Sheffield it was George Caborn at Firth Brown Tools and Les Ambrose at Shardlow's. Often these conveners tended, though not always, to be members of the AEU rather than the TGWU but, in what were very diversified workplaces in terms of union memberships, they held their positions because they could command cross-union support.[14]

There was a reason for this. It is one that partly explains the more general shift to the Left in these years. Those on the Left stood for the general principle of industrial unionism and for reducing differentials. The Left had, since the 1920s, fought for equal pay for equal work, for 100 per cent trade unionism and against divisions on the basis of race or, in Scotland, Merseyside and Ireland, of religion. The politics of the Right tended to be different and based on defending differentials and exclusions.

11 MRC MSS 684/5/4, 1961 Biennial Conference: Agenda.

12 Paul Smith, 'The Transformation of the Transport and General Workers' Union: The Dunlop Dispute, 1961', *HSIR*, 2008, vol.25–26, no.1, pp.219–238.

13 Jack Dash, *Good Morning Brothers* (London, Mayflower 1970), pp.76 and 82.

14 R. Seifert and T. Sibley, *Revolutionary Communist at Work: A Political Biography of Bert Ramelson* (Lawrence and Wishart, 2012; J. McIlroy, '"Every Factory Our Fortress": Communist Party Workplace Branches in a Time of Militancy, 1956–79, Part 2: Testimonies and Judgements', *HSIR*, 2001, vol.12, no.1, pp.57–107; Davie Cooper, former convener Govan Yard, interview by John Foster, 2019, Unite Oral History Archive, 128 Theobalds Road, London WC1X 8TN, contact Jim Mowatt.

The strength of the Right lay in trade identity and sometimes religious identity. In the post-war period such trade sectionalism could be effective: driving up wages trade by trade. But it was increasingly trumped in the massive plants and combines of the 1960s by the potential gains from workplace unity. And it was Lefts in skilled jobs who could best build this unity between skilled and semi-skilled grades. They could hold the confidence of their fellow skilled workers while securing the wider workplace unity needed to put management on the defensive and deprive them of the usual tactic of playing off one section against the other.

There was, however, another and equally important reason for the shift to the Left in the 1960s. This was the increasingly aggressive intervention by government to curb the freedom of shop stewards to initiate strike action. To understand why governments intervened in this way we have to examine the wider political economy of post-war Britain, a place that, looking back now, seems like a foreign country.

Britain As a Foreign Country

In 1960 Britain was still the centre of a vast empire. Almost a million soldiers were under arms to defend a network of colonies and neo-colonies that spanned the globe. The giant companies and banks that dominated Britain's domestic economy derived much of their income from the oil fields spread across the captive sheikdoms and monarchies of the Middle East, from the copper, gold, bauxite, uranium and zinc extracted from Central Africa, Kenya and Guyana and rubber, coffee and tea traded through Malaya, Singapore and Hong Kong. These firms – BP, Shell, Unilever, Rio Tinto, Anglo-American, Pearson, Jardine Mathieson – were closely interlocked with the City of London's merchant banks.[15] So also were others such as Rolls Royce, ICI, Hawker Siddeley, De Haviland and Vickers, which formed a state-supported military-industrial complex that still gave Britain world leadership in some areas of technology, notably supersonic flight and nuclear fission.[16] By 1960, however, the costs of this empire-based economy had become unsustainable, both economically and, after Britain's forced withdrawal from Suez, politically. It was in response to this crisis that Harold Macmillan's Conservative government attempted a transition to new policies based on a programme of large-scale industrial modernisation to match developments in Germany, Japan and France. It was the way these policies were implemented that led to the stand-off with the trade union movement.

15 B. Tew, *Studies in Company Finance* (Cambridge University Press, 1959); S. Aaronovitch, *Studies in British Monopoly Capitalism* (Lawrence and Wishart, 1955).
16 The National Archives (hereafter TNA) CAB 124 100/21, Sandys to Cabinet, 9 February 1960: subsidies required to consolidate Britain's military aircraft sector.

The dominant explanation blamed trade unionists for the irresponsible abuse of the strike weapon to push up wages. Such action, it was claimed, menaced both economic growth and the welfare state and violated the consensus agreed by Labour and the Conservatives at the end of the war – requiring governments to intervene to prevent a return to the mass unemployment of the 1930s.

The Left, however, took a different position. William Beveridge's call for 'full employment in a free society' was, they argued, fairly consciously posed against 'state socialism' in Eastern Europe and more broadly against socialism in general.[17] Beveridge, a Liberal – and as a senior civil servant responsible for deporting the Clydeside shop stewards in 1916 – argued that a generous system of social insurance was itself enough to avoid future slumps. No further social change was needed – certainly not socialism. By redistributing income across generations and between the employed and the unemployed, demand and employment would be maintained. In turn another Liberal, Maynard Keynes, claimed that the new post-war system of managed currencies also made it possible to control economic cycles. As the main architect of the 1944 Bretton Woods Agreement with the United States, which initiated the International Monetary Fund, Keynes claimed that injecting extra cash into the economy specifically to stimulate demand, and hence production, could maintain business confidence without causing inflation. This was because the extra goods produced would soak up the additional cash in a 'multiplier' effect. The only problem, warned Keynes, would be if trade unionists abused their position. Exploiting full employment to push for unreasonable wage demands would indeed create inflation and destabilise the whole system.[18]

At the time, in the 1940s, left-wing economists had warned of the dangers of these arguments. Expanding the money supply was itself

---

17 William Beveridge, *Full Employment in a Free Society* (Norton, 1945).

18 The wartime and immediate post-war debates on the class orientation of Keynesian economics are examined in J. Foster, 'Labour, Keynesianism and the Welfare State', in J. Fyrth (ed.), *Labour's High Noon 1945–1951* (Lawrence and Wishart, 1993). Tim Claydon, 'Tales of Disorder in the Press and the Narrative Construction of Industrial Relations in the British Motor Industry, 1950–79', *HSIR*, 2000, vol.9, no.1, pp.1–36, examines the use of the Keynesian economic narrative in the 1950s and 1960s – although Claydon was probably not then aware of the now more clearly exposed role of security service briefings to both the BBC (especially Panorama) and the press. W. Styles, 'British Domestic Security Policy and Communist Subversion', PhD thesis (Cambridge University, 2016) pp.120 ff. Styles documents cooperation between MI5, the government's secret anti-communist Information Research Department and the BBC from 1957 in a campaign to destabilise communist influence in the ETU – with the Cabinet Committee on Communism (Home) congratulating itself after the end of the ETU trial in 1960 that no evidence of its involvement had become public: 'Communism in the Trade Unions', Foreign Office to Communism (Home)', TNA CAB 134/1345, 21 November 1960.

inflationary but it would be particularly so in Britain where monopolies and cartels dominated so much of the economy. The new ideology of 'managed capitalism' promoted by Keynes and Beveridge would put the blame on workers and justify government intervention in wage bargaining. Worse still would be its wider political consequences. If accepted in the labour movement, it would draw both Labour Party and trade union leaders into policing wage demands and put them into conflict with their members trying to defend living standards. In doing so it would cripple the labour movement's wider potential for genuine social change.[19]

Volume III has shown that this is exactly what happened after 1945. The ideology of managed capitalism was used to justify quite draconian action against unofficial strikes and within the TGWU to defend Deakin's rigid centralisation of power. In the 1960s these claims became even more strident. Newspaper columnists, academics, royal commissions and mass circulation films and novels portrayed 'I'm alright Jack' shop stewards as blocking industrial modernisation.

Frank Cousins Challenges Right-wing Economics

By contrast, Frank Cousins defied these claims. He argued that the causes of Britain's crisis did indeed result from the closed, monopolistic nature of the British economy, its political and economic dependence on the US and the lack of any control over profits and how they were invested. Writing in the *Record* for February 1962 Cousins attacked the Conservative government for simply seeking to boost exports by curbing domestic demand – which, in practice, meant attacking the living standards of his members. 'We need real planning with teeth able to direct industry as firmly as the government has tried to direct wages'. 'It is only by intervening in the 80 per cent of the economy which is privately controlled that a real solution of our economic problems can be found'.[20]

Cousins's arguments were founded in the contrasting economic analysis now being advanced with growing force and relevance by left-wing economists such as Maurice Dobb, Michael Barrett Brown and Sam Aaronovitch. These authors provided a key armoury for trade unionists in debate and negotiation.[21] As in the 1940s they argued that it was Keynesian

19 Jim Fyrth (ed.), *Labour's High Noon: The Government and the Economy* (Lawrence and Wishart, 1993), pp.20–25, examines the critique advanced by Maurice Dobb and others in the 1940s.

20 TGWU *Record*, February 1962.

21 M. Dobb, *Capitalism Today and Yesterday* (Lawrence and Wishart, 1960); Sam Aaronovitch, *The Ruling Class: A Study of British Finance Capital* (Lawrence and Wishart, 1961) and *Economics for Trade Unionists* (Lawrence and Wishart, 1964); M. Barratt Brown, *After Imperialism* (Heineman, 1963).

cash expansion and domestic monopolisation that caused inflation. They pointed out that Britain had ended the war with a domestic economy relatively unscathed compared with those in continental Europe and Japan. Partly as a result, the post-war Labour government's export drive was notably successful. By 1950 Britain was manufacturing 20 per cent of all global exports and almost 40 per cent of all motor vehicle exports. US manufacturers, Ford, General Motors and Chrysler, invested in Britain to secure cheaper labour and exported the cars back into the US, making up a third of all motor exports in the early 1950s. Yet by 1960 this lead had been lost and British industry was being comprehensively outpaced by Germany and Japan, in large measure because these countries had repeatedly devalued their currencies. Britain had not devalued, partly because of the 1944 link with the dollar and partly because British companies and investors still enjoyed the benefits of empire and of internal monopolisation.[22]

The scale of Britain's monopolisation was indeed massive. It was exposed in the 1960s by the work of the Monopolies Commission.[23] Four companies controlled 95 per cent of car output. Glass for the windows was almost exclusively manufactured by Pilkington, a private company making 40 per cent profits through most of the 1960s. Motor electrics were controlled by Joseph Lucas and tyres largely by Dunlop. Elsewhere the market for oil and petrol was dominated by four firms. ICI controlled industrial chemicals and Courtaulds artificial fibres and textiles. The same also applied to the retail sector. Five big supermarkets dominated.[24]

The Politics of the Sterling–Dollar Link and Macmillan's Policy Shift

There was, however, another equally important dimension to this monopolised economy which, the Left argued, derived from Britain's legacy as an imperial power and the international alliances this required.

Monopolisation in Britain was linked to the dominance of companies, BP, ICI, Dunlop, Lucas and Unilever, mainly devoted to the extraction, manufacturing and marketing of colonial commodities. Both internal and

22 Jack Saunders, 'The British Motor Industry 1945–77: How Workplace Culture Shaped Workplace Militancy', PhD thesis (University College London, 2015) provides the background to much of the subsequent discussion.
23 Monopolies Commission, *A Study of Mergers 1958–68* (HMSO, 1970). Edward Heath, as president of the Board of Trade in 1963 privately admitted the scale of monopolistic price control in his paper to the Cabinet: Helen Mercer, 'The Abolition of Retail Price Maintenance in Britain in 1964', LSE Working Paper in Economic History, 39/98, January 1998.
24 The government was well aware of these problems: TNA CAB 129 105/44, Selwyn Lloyd to Cabinet 10 July 1961. 'Economic Growth and National Efficiency'.

external monopolies were interlocked with the London merchant banks which historically controlled the flow of capital overseas. Through their dominant links with the Bank of England (they composed its board of governors) they possessed a key influence over monetary policy. And it was this that underlay Britain's ambiguous and sometimes conflictual relationship with the United States.[25]

The Keynesian Bretton Woods Agreement of 1944 enabled both the US, and Britain on a smaller scale, to expand their currency issue to maintain global demand (effectively for the goods they themselves manufactured by lending money to debtor countries). At the same time the dollar (and through its link to the dollar, the pound) remained pegged to gold at $35 an ounce – on the Keynesian assumption that if economies grew, no inflation should occur. For Britain this expansion in sterling liquidity, lent at interest to 'developing' countries and colonies, had been a significant factor in its immediate post-war export boom. The same process, administered through the World Bank and the International Monetary Fund (IMF), was even more important for clinching US dominance of the world market.

However, this sterling–dollar link became increasingly problematic – complicated and deepened by the politics of war and decolonisation. The US wanted access to British colonial markets and used its wartime and post-war aid, and the massive dollar debts that resulted, to demand an end to any formal or informal protection through tariffs or monetary controls. At the same time it wanted Britain to bear the costs of colonial defence and combatting communist insurgency. And it did so at time of heightened international confrontation with the USSR and socialist China as joint US-British forces battled to contain liberation struggles stretching from Korea, Malaya and Indo-China to the Philippines and Indonesia, across the Middle East from Iran to Egypt and, increasingly, in Africa and Latin America.

The US itself paid for much of the resulting military expenditure by printing dollars – still valued at 1944 parity. This made the US, and the US international banks, extremely hostile to any proposal by Britain to devalue its own currency. Such devaluation would undermine the credibility of the dollar's own link with gold. Equally difficult for Britain's governing elite was the American insistence that Britain maintain its defence expenditure, including its very costly involvements in the Far East, while at the same time reserving the right to block any attempt by Britain to exercise an independent role, as at Suez.

Harold Macmillan's new policies of 1960–1961 were a response to this crisis, to the decline of Britain's exports and the consequent threat

---

25 Barratt Brown, *After Imperialism* was an important contemporary source for this analysis.

to the balance of payments and the City of London. Macmillan opted for the same policies of state-aided amalgamation as France, Germany and Japan based on the creation of giant, though privately owned, industrial corporations. In the process Britain would abandon the formal military and political control of its colonies – though maintaining its central role in the North Atlantic Treaty Organization (NATO) as a nuclear power – and seek membership of the Common Market to expand access to Europe.

And how would this be paid for? As in the past, argued the economists of the Left, by working people. Wages would be held down as inflation increased.

It was this political context that made the TGWU's 1960 intervention in the Labour Party so dramatic and important. By reasserting Clause 4 it argued that the current crisis could not be resolved on the terms set by big business. The move to socialist control of industry was, as Frank Cousins argued, not a pious ambition but an urgent necessity. Similarly, when Frank Cousins opposed nuclear weapons, he was attacking what he saw as the basis of Britain's economically debilitating, and politically immoral, nuclear pact with the US and doing so at a time of sharply increasing global tension.

Hence, if we are to explain the changing politics of the shop floor during the 1960s it is this additional element that must be added. It was not just organisation and the creation of a new level of shop steward coordination across companies at national level. It was also politics – the argument and discussion that took place on the shop floor. The Left's emphasis on workplace unity and 100 per cent trade unionism was important. But equally important were the wider political arguments of the Left. In face of increasing legal intervention to stop shop-floor strike action, shop stewards on the Left were able to demonstrate why this was being done – exposing the empty rhetoric of the government and the press. Its real rationale and purpose was an immoral and highly dangerous battle to maintain world control.

Big Business Moves into Action: Harvesting Cheaper Regional Labour

On 16 April 1960 Cousins wrote in his diary: 'Met Sir Patrick Hennessy of Fords at his flat to discuss the agreement he has reached with the AEU and National Union of General and Municipal Workers (NUGMW) re separate and less expensive wages and conditions agreement covering the new plant which the company are to develop on Merseyside. Suggested to Sir P that this would not be acceptable to other unions and that he should reconsider his position and put the subject back for discussion at the National Negotiating Committee of Fords'. He continued 'Apparently some union leaders are prepared to buy their way into the new factories by agreeing to things which cannot work. Some employers will no doubt favour doing business with Bill Carron [general secretary of the engineering union] who is willing to be tolerant and cooperative and is anti-CP'.[26]

This was the real economic face of Macmillan's plan to develop industrial giants that could compete with Germany and Japan. It was to be done by cutting wages and exploiting the much higher levels of unemployment that the government had allowed to develop on Merseyside, Wales, the North East and Scotland – pitting worker against worker.[27] Already the government had laid the basis by a massive closure of capacity in the state-owned coal and rail industries between 1958 and 1960. In both industries employment was to be reduced by up to a third with the losses concentrated in the north and west.[28] Conscription was also ended – pushing another 300,000 into the labour market.[29] Unemployment increased from 1.6 per cent in 1961 to 2.1 per cent in 1962 and 2.6 per cent in 1963.[30]

Even in the Midlands this was beginning to have an impact. In his September quarterly report for 1961 Jack Jones wrote: 'Midlands industry has been hit disastrously by the Chancellor of the Exchequer's new credit squeeze and the fall in exports. On every hand there is evidence of short-time working and redundancy and it is clear that the situation will grow worse in the next few months'. Earlier in April 1960 Jones had reported on the moves by Ford to shift production to the north: 'Due to unilateral action by the AEU, which came to my attention, I contacted the General Secretary and subsequently a conference took place of regional secretaries concerned with the new developments. Since that conference I have assisted in making contacts for the Scottish and Liverpool regional secretaries'.[31] One outcome was the conference that Dick Etheridge attended on 15 September 1960 representing Longbridge workers.

By then it had become clear that this was not just about Ford. It was general policy. The government was in discussion with firms across the motor industry, in aviation and electrical engineering. Jones himself reported that he had had discussions with 'Mr G Harriman of the BMC

---

26 MRC MSS 282/8/1/1, Cousins's diary, 16 April 1960.

27 TNA CAB 129/100/15, Maudling to Cabinet, 7 February 1960, discusses the issue of how many firms could be directed to Merseyside without unduly depleting the labour surplus and affecting wage rates.

28 TNA CAB 129 101/3, Macmillan to Cabinet, 16 March 1960, discusses the Guillibaud Report on rails and the consequent release of labour.

29 TNA CAB 129 100/4, Watkinson (Defence) to Cabinet, 6 February 1960, on the labour market consequences of the release of 300,000 national service conscripts.

30 Jon Murden, 'Demands for Fair Wages and Pay Parity in the British Motor Industry in the 1960s and 1970s', *HSIR*, 2005, vol.20, no.1, pp.1–27.

31 MRC MSS 126/TG/101/1/1, Region 5 minutes 1960–61, for April and September 1960 and January 1961.

on their proposed development at Swinnerton (near Stoke on Trent)'. Rootes, BMC, General Motors – as well as other big firms outside the motor industry – were relocating new plants away from the South East with the objective of playing off regional differentials. As Jack Jones explained, there were general principles at stake in terms of working-class unity. 'On the one hand we have to ensure that pockets of unemployment don't arise here as a result of taking jobs elsewhere. On the other hand, there is need to ensure strong trade union organisation in the new factories (preferably in this union) so as to maintain good standards of wages and working conditions'. By the following summer, June 1961, Jones was underlining his concern at the 'transference of jobs to the new factories of the Merseyside and Scotland. Ahead of us looms the prospect of a great economic crisis with the government determined to make the work people bear most of the burden. This is typical of the capitalist approach'.[32] These were also the arguments that the Left were putting on the shop floor. The 'capitalist approach' was to make workers pay for the new investment and to use it to divide the trade union movement.

So, if a shift in Left–Right allegiances did occur in the course of the decade, it was not simply that Left stewards and conveners could deliver better economic outcomes using strategies of workplace unity. It was the result of how day-to-day events were explained. Shop-floor discussion was crucial. The capitalist approach, the Left argued, was about the accumulation of wealth at the expense of those who created it. The government's new drive for 'planning' had little to do with using the full potential of modern science to transform industry itself. It had a great deal to do with reasserting control over labour.

This understanding of the 'capitalist approach' was also why Frank Cousins decided to intervene more directly in the Labour Party, as we will see in the two following chapters.

32 MRC MSS 126/TG/101/1/1, Region 5 minutes 1960–61, June 1961.

2

'The Public Ownership of the Means of Production, Distribution and Exchange'

In which Frank Cousins defeats Labour's right wing and asserts public ownership as the only way to harness scientific potential and reverse industrial decline

Heathrow

Heathrow became Britain's main international airport in1946. It did so as the headquarters of the British Overseas Airways Corporation (BOAC), formed at the beginning of the war as a public corporation and fully nationalised in 1946. The airport became the shop window for Britain's advanced technology. The world's first jet airliner, the de Haviland Comet, took off from Heathrow in May 1952 – to South Africa. The world's first supersonic airliner, Concorde, took off from Heathrow in January 1976 – to Bahrain.

Employment at the airport rose from a little over 1,000 in 1946 to 26,000 by the late 1950s and was well in excess of 30,000 by the mid-1960s. In the 1920s the wider area had been open countryside just 20 miles west of London. By the 1930s it had become the base for a range of engineering and consumer goods factories. Its villages became towns. The great majority of the workers in these pre-war factories were immigrants – from inner London, from those English regions where interwar unemployment had been particularly high and also from Wales and rural Ireland. In the 1940s and 1950s new immigrants arrived from India, mainly Sikhs from Punjab.[1]

---

1 Barbara Humphries, 'Origin and Development of the Labour Movement in West London, 1918–70', PhD thesis (University of Reading, 2018).

It was from this population that Heathrow's new workforce was drawn. During the 1930s, but particularly during the war, there had been a largely successful drive to unionise the expanding engineering factories. At the same time there was a drive by the Left to overcome quite serious ethnic divisions, particularly discrimination in jobs and housing, against workers from Wales and Ireland. In the 1945 election, though less so in the 1950s, the Labour Party had been successful. By and large it worked in tandem with the Communist Party which had industrial branches in 20 of the local factories. During and immediately after the war the principle of 100 per cent unionisation had largely been won across West Middlesex.

By the 1960s most departments in Heathrow airport itself were 100 per cent unionised and the TGWU had become the airport's biggest union, with roughly 5,000 members working alongside a range of other unions: the engineers, draughtsmen, Association of Scientific, Technical and Managerial Staffs (ASTMS) and pilots in British Airline Pilots Association (BALPA). Rather like in assembly-line factories, an airport provided workers with significant opportunities for quick on-the-job industrial action – such as the lighting strike by engineers on 15 January 1960. A more major confrontation came in March 1961 when the TGWU led a thousand maintenance workers in a three-week strike against a new supervisory system, a strike which resulted in a significant advance in pay and conditions.[2] A further strike by baggage handlers followed in November, also resulting in a considerable pay increase.[3] These strikes were particularly significant because at this point almost all workers at Heathrow were government employees – air transport being then nationalised – and it was through its control of public sector employment that the government was seeking to enforce its wage freeze. However, faced with the bargaining strength of airport workers, the management found it expedient simply to regrade all the workers involved at higher wages and better conditions.[4]

By the early1970s, with John Cousins as local organiser, the TGWU's membership stood at 15,000. It was the dominant union in a workplace in which 100 per cent trade unionism was largely mandatory. The workplace branch of the Communist Party had over a hundred members and was described as being highly influential across all the airport's unions.[5] By then Heathrow had become another fortress of the working-class movement.

It was therefore possibly not altogether accidental that in 1964–1965 Heathrow was the site of one of the most lethal legal attacks on the trade

2 *Daily Worker*, 16 January 1960; Ministry of Labour *Gazette*, April 1961.
3 Ministry of Labour *Gazette*, November 1961.
4 MRC MSS 126/TG/1186/A/39, GEC minutes, December 1961.
5 Humphries, 'Origin and Development of the Labour Movement'.

union movement last century – precisely over the principle of 100 per cent trade unionism: the Rookes-Barnard legal judgement.

Douglas Rookes worked in the BOAC design office at Heathrow. In 1964 he took it upon himself to resign from his union, Association of Engineering and Shipbuilding Draughtsmen (AESD) (later Technical Administrative and Supervisory Section, TASS) which had a 100 per cent membership agreement with BOAC. The union threatened strike action and Rookes was dismissed by BOAC. Rookes then took his case to law suing the union branch chair, his shop steward and the divisional organiser. At the first hearing he won the case, then had it overturned on appeal and then took it to the House of Lords. There Lord Devlin gave his judgement against the union. The threat of strike action represented, he said, unlawful intimidation and hence invited unlimited damages – thereby opening any strike action, or threat of it, to prosecution. The TUC quickly brought pressure on the Labour government to pass the 1965 Trades Disputes Act. But the case itself reflected the growing determination within sections of big business and the judiciary to confront trade union power.

To understand why big business and its allies within the state machine were moving in this much more confrontational direction we also need to understand how far, during previous five years, the Left in the trade union movement had successfully challenged the existing pro-business status quo – with Frank Cousins and the TGWU being the leading force.

1960: Cousins Defeats the Labour Party Right Wing

On 26 March 1960 Cousins wrote in his diary:

> The Labour Party NEC gave consideration to revision of Party aims. However much subsequent events are used to disguise this, it has become an attempt by Hugh Gaitskell and his intimates [...] to create in the minds of the electorate, particularly the 'reform' type of person, that the Labour Party has abandoned its belief in nationalisation as a basic and essential part of a socialist economy. They are determined to sacrifice *our* principles for the sake of securing an election victory. The importance of this move is that the particular group of politicians of the Gaitskell, Crosland, Wyatt, Jay, Callaghan, Gordon Walker type are really trying to secure the removal from the constitution of the Labour Party the reference to those aspects of policy in which they *do not have* any belief. They are reformists with a main purpose of securing power for themselves, quite happy to maintain the existing structure of society.[6]

6   MRC MSS 282/8/1/1, F. Cousins, diary entry for 6 December 1959.

It was the intervention by the TGWU at the Labour Party National Executive Committee (NEC), made by its representative Harry Nicholas, that forced the right wing to abandon its attempt to remove the existing socialist Clause 4 from the constitution. Instead, a face-saving 'commentary' was adopted for the forthcoming Labour Party conference. By autumn even this was abandoned. By then Gaitskell and his allies faced an even bigger challenge: the reversal of the Labour Party's existing commitment to nuclear weapons.

Cousins had personally supported the Campaign for Nuclear Disarmament (CND) since its foundation in 1957 and had joined the Aldermaston marches. In 1959 he had helped win the union's biennial conference to opposition to Britain's use of nuclear weapons. The resolution argued that basing defence policy on the threat to use nuclear weapons was 'morally wrong, militarily dangerous and economically unsound'.[7] Now the TGWU proposed to take this policy position to the Labour Party conference and do so with the support of the engineers who, much to the anger of its right-wing leadership, had adopted similar policy. In doing so, the two unions were giving support to the traditional position of the left wing of the Labour Party and until very recently also of Aneurin Bevan. To the consternation of Gaitskell and the party leadership, conference supported the motion – despite manoeuvres by the engineer's general secretary Bill Carron and an attempt by Hugh Gaitskell to turn the issue into a motion of confidence.

Why did such a 'non-industrial issue' assume such importance for Cousins and the TGWU? There were probably two reasons. First, the scale of the public concern at the escalation of Cold War tensions in 1958–1960 – with Britain in the front line, and second, the degree to which Cousins and the Left saw Gaitskell's support for these policies as closely linked to attempts to shift the party to the right and to abandon socialism.

The failure of Britain's Blue Streak missile system in 1958–1959 had forced Harold Macmillan to negotiate use of the US's submarine-based Polaris missiles. In return Britain was being asked to strengthen its own armed presence in the Far East, to support German rearmament and allow the basing of US submarines in the Holy Loch in Scotland – enabling the US to launch nuclear strikes from waters far closer to the USSR. This represented a new stage in the nuclear arms race and one in which Britain was both in the front line and no longer fully in control of its own nuclear weapons.

These were the policies that Gaitskell backed and he did so at a time of rapidly increasing international tension. In the Far East, January 1960

---

7 Geoffrey Goodman, *The Awkward Warrior, Frank Cousins: His Life and Times* (Davis-Poynter, 1979), pp.200–234.

Figure 2: Frank Cousins and Canon John Collins leading the
1959 Aldermaston march
(Unite Photo Archive, 128 Theobalds Road, London WC1X 8TN,
contact Jim Mowatt)

saw the first major engagement of US forces in Vietnam. In May 1960, America's U2 spy plane was shot down over Russia while mapping nuclear targets. In Africa the US was in the process of overthrowing Patrice Lumumba, the newly elected leader of the Democratic People's Republic (DPR) of Congo and in the Americas the US was taking an increasingly hostile stance against the new left-wing government in Cuba.

At the same time it was also quite apparent that the same forces supporting Gaitskell's pro-nuclear policy were also the driving force behind the moves to remove Clause 4. In 1958 the German social democrats adopted the Godesberg programme that ended any formal commitment to socialism – on the grounds that the party could never win an election while so committed.[8] After the 1959 election Penguin published the mass circulation *Must Labour Lose?* by Mark Abrams, Rita Hinden and Richard Rose, making similar arguments for Britain.[9] In both cases we now know that the advocates of these changes were heavily funded by US agencies and foundations. The Ford and Rockefeller foundations and the state department provided much of the finance required to fund the publications, staffing and international travel of Gaitskell and the Labour Party's right wing. At least some of this was known at the time to Cousins and his supporters in the Labour Party.[10] Interviewed in September 1960, prior to the conference vote, Cousins made clear that he saw nuclear disarmament and the defence of the party's socialist objectives as closely linked.

> Mr Cousins stresses that the clash on nuclear weapons is not the only problem facing the labour and trade union movement, though he believes it epitomises deeply conflicting attitudes on other vital issues. Public ownership is the most outstanding and here it should be remembered that right-wing Labour and trade union leaders have clearly said they oppose its extension. There Mr Cousins regards the issue in the movement as between those who desire Socialism and those who do not. This is the key to the struggle now taking place.[11]

The dual defeat for Gaitskell was therefore an issue of major concern for the US state department. US relations with the ruling Conservative Party had not been good, with repeated clashes over colonial resources. Most recently in 1960 there had been strongly divergent policies over the fate of the DPR Congo and its reserves of uranium and copper.[12] There was much annoyance at the British failure to endorse US policy in Vietnam. There was also disquiet over Macmillan's approach to the European Community. The availability of an alternative government in the form of a politically reliable social democratic party had, as in Western Germany, been seen as a major policy objective. Frank Cousins was identified as instrumental in blocking this outcome. In August 1960 Alex Kitson,

---

8 W. Paterson, 'Re-programming Democratic Socialism', *West European Politics*, volume 16/1, 1993.

9 M. Abrams, R. Hinden and R. Rose, *Must Labour Lose?* (Penguin, 1959).

10 Lawrence Black, '"The Bitterest Enemies of Communism": Labour Revisionists, Atlanticism and the Cold War', *Contemporary British History*, 2001, vol.15, no.3, pp.26–72; Carl Hodge, 'The Long Fifties: The Politics of Socialist Programmatic Revision in Britain, France and Germany', *Contemporary European History*, 1993, vol.2, no.1, pp.17–34.

11 Cousins interviewed in the *Daily Worker*, 19 September 1960.

12 Steve Marsh and Tia Culley, 'Anglo-American Relations and Crisis in The Congo', *Contemporary British History*, 2018, vol.32, no.3, pp.359–384.

general secretary of the Scottish Commercial Motormen, reported from the Berne conference of the International Transport Workers Federation, after Cousins's summary removal as chair of the federation, that this had been planned over dinner at the US embassy following a telegram from the state department.[13]

But Cousins's own objective was different. It was not to spite the Americans. It was to ensure that the Labour Party could indeed enact the policies needed to safeguard Britain's productive resources for working people.

TGWU Stands Firm Against Wage Cuts: Tory Industrial Strategy Starts to Fall Apart

As we have seen, a key part of Conservative Party policy for industrial redevelopment was the control of labour costs. Partly, it was hoped that market forces themselves could achieve this – by releasing labour from state-controlled industries, shifting production to development regions and enabling a limited rise in unemployment overall. Partly, it was hoped that it could be achieved by the kind of understandings with the TUC and union leaders that had existed in the post-war period under the Labour government. At the very outset of his new policies in 1958, Macmillan had established a council on production, prices and incomes to which he hoped to attract the TUC leaders, and for this reason it was to be independent and non-governmental. However, in this objective it failed – partly because of Cousins's opposition – and by 1960 the Cabinet was discussing letting it die a natural death.[14]

Wages nonetheless remained a central preoccupation and attention focused increasingly on unofficial strikes. In May 1961 the Minister of Labour, John Hare, reported to Cabinet that the preceding 12 months had seen few major official strikes but a very large number of unofficial strikes concentrated in four industries: shipbuilding, motors, docks and coal.[15] He singled out motors. With just 1.7 per cent of the labour force it accounted for 17 per cent of lost time. In the context of discussions with Frank Cousins he stressed the need to look for cooperation with the unions in improving industrial relations' management rather than any legislative

13 This was the front page story in the *Daily Worker* on 2 August 1960.

14 TNA CAB 129 100/40, Heathcote Amery, 4 February 1960. Peter Dorey, '"Don't Intervene": The Conservative Party's *Voluntaristic* Approach to Industrial Relations and Trade Unionism, 1951–1964', *Contemporary British History*, 2018, vol.32, no.3, pp.406–436 stresses the reluctance to directly challenge the 'official' leadership of the trade union movement throughout.

15 TNA CAB 129 105/14, John Hare to Cabinet, 15 May 1961.

intervention. Hare also stressed the need to make effective use of the 'ETU case' to combat communist influence.[16]

Over the following three years the country's economic performance continued to deteriorate relative to its trading rivals. Exports failed to fill the sterling deficit. Pressures mounted from the IMF and the US for reductions in consumption and imports – fearful of the effects of any sterling devaluation on the dollar. In February 1962 the chancellor, Selwyn Lloyd, was warning that state spending projections to 1964 were unsustainable in face of the dollar deficit and labour shortages.[17]. He tried and failed to get TUC backing for a 2.5 per cent 'guiding light' at a time when inflation was running at 4.3 per cent.[18] Thereafter the government's options were limited. Short of legally imposing wage restrictions, the only way it could directly influence wage settlements was in the public sector. But here it ran directly into conflict with Frank Cousins and the TGWU who organised many of the workers – in road haulage, buses, airports, electricity supply and the docks, where the publicly owned Transport Commission was the biggest employer. Attempts to impose limits resulted in a ragged series of strikes and threats of strikes and had only very limited effect.

The dockers put up the most determined resistance, with the threat of a total strike by 63,000 registered dock workers across the country. Frank Cousins made it clear that the union would not condone an effective pay cut and would use all its resources to resist. On 8 May 1962 Reginald Maudling briefed the Cabinet on the option of employing scabs or the armed forces in the docks and on the problems likely to result in terms of public opinion and more general relations with the trade unions.[19] On 13 May, the day before the strike was due to begin, the port employers capitulated. It was, as Jack Dash commented, the first occasion since the war that all dockers had been united and been backed by their union.[20] The following January, in the face of strike action by electricity supply workers, again including TGWU members, the postmaster general Henry Brooke reported that the ministerial committee on emergencies had concluded that it would not be wise to introduce legislation to restrict strike action. It was thought 'better to concentrate on a) positive steps to make workers in the industry more responsible, and b) discreet exposure of communist activity. As to a) the Minister of Power has now concluded that in his view it would not be practicable to include a provision banning strikes in the

---

16 TNA CAB 129 105/14, Hare to Cabinet, 15 May 1961; Styles, 'British Domestic Security Policy'.

17 TNA CAB 129 108/27, Selwyn Lloyd to Cabinet, 13 February 1962.

18 TNA CAB 129 108/1.1, Selwyn Lloyd to Cabinet, 10 January 1962.

19 TNA CAB 129 109/16, Maudling to Cabinet, 8 May 1962.

20 Dash, *Good Morning, Brothers*, p.112.

proposed scheme for raising the status of workers in the industry. As to b) action is proceeding'.[21]

Six months later the TGWU's 1963 biennial conference reaffirmed opposition to any attempts to enforce pay restraint through the public sector and noted its 'disastrous effects on industrial relations'. It was agreed to 'progressively move forward on the basis of the industrial negotiation related to the economic strength of the union'. 'Whilst profits and prices remain uncontrolled conference declares that the strength of the Union must be used to implement a wages strategy based on reasonable wage demands and a progressive reduction of the working week'.[22]

Following the failure of the government's attempt to win support from the TUC for an 'independent' incomes commission, Macmillan then attempted to meet TUC concerns by creating a National Economic Development Council (NEDC) focused on the planned development of industrial potential and with no remit to discuss wages. Cousins reluctantly agreed to join on these terms. But the NEDC soon got bogged down in disputes between employers wanting a speedier rundown in the public sector employment and the unions pushing for legislation on redundancy.[23] Meanwhile, as the balance of payments deteriorated and the scale of unofficial strikes increased, the government found itself caught between Conservative backbenchers demanding new laws banning such strikes and a TUC opposed to legislative intervention.[24]

In these circumstances sections of corporate business, particularly as represented by the Confederation of British Industry (CBI), began to look to the Labour Party as a more effective vehicle for resolving the growing crisis.[25]

Cousins Re-engages With the Labour Party Leadership: For a Planned Economy – but What Kind?

It was clear to those in the leadership of the Labour Party that if the party was to offer an alternative government in these circumstances it had to get

21 TNA CAB 129 111/7, Henry Brooke to Cabinet, 23 January 1963.
22 MRC MSS 126/TG/1887/20, 1963 Biennial Conference, 9 July 1963, minute no. 27.
23 TNA CAB 129 113/31, Maudling to Cabinet, 26 February 1963.
24 TNA CAB 129 117/1, Godber, Minister of Labour, 18 February 1964, on half of all days lost through unofficial strikes; TNA CAB 129 11711, 4 March 1964, on clash with both backbenchers and TUC.
25 Keith Middlemas, *Power, Competition and the State: Threats to the Post-war Settlement Britain 1961–74*, vol. 2 (Macmillan, 1990) pp.80 ff provides general background. Samuel Brittan, *The Treasury under the Tories 1951–64* (Penguin, 1964) would be one example of a call to Labour.

the trade union movement on board – and in particular secure the support of Frank Cousins, the dominant figure on the Left. The question was what kind of government and what kind of policies.

In the autumn of 1962 Gaitskell himself approached Cousins after a period in which both had opposed, though for somewhat different reasons, Macmillan's bid to join the European Community. After the 1962 Labour Party conference, where Cousins had supported Gaitskell on Europe, Gaitskell made his approach. Cousins was equivocal. Three months later Gaitskell died and Cousins backed Wilson, the apparent inheritor of Aneurin Bevan's radicalism, against George Brown, Gaitskell's deputy. In the run up to the 1963 Labour Party conference, a year ahead of the general election, Wilson himself approached Cousins.

As recounted in Cousins's diary, the meeting was initiated on the basis

> of a frank discussion on the economic problems facing the country and the need to deal realistically with the whole range of economic planning including education and the scientific issues [...] in addition to the role of NEDC. I maintained the view previously expressed that Planning was a function of government and therefore that the NEDC under Labour must be very closely associated with a government department and could not function adequately on a purely voluntary or 'planning by consent' basis. There appeared to be a need for a ministry of economic affairs or planning – not the Treasury or Chancellor's department.[26]

Wilson suggested that Cousins might want to take the Board of Trade or Ministry of Transport. Cousins indicated initially that he 'already had a sufficiently important job as General Secretary of the TGWU' and 'any Labour prime minister needed someone strong in support within the unions'. Later, however, he conceded that he would 'enjoy the challenge of the position of Min of Transport but only if it was recognised as part of the planning function, that he would have Wilson's support and that it would be a Cabinet level position'.[27]

During the conference itself Wilson asked Cousins to come into debate to support him when he sought to open a new perspective for a Labour government – seeking to identify with the 'white heat' of the 'technological and scientific revolution'. He also asked Cousins to intervene in a second debate on 'economic planning and incomes policy', to make clear his position and to liaise beforehand with Jim Callaghan who was replying. This Cousins did and noted Callaghan's responses.

26 MRC MSS 282/8/3/2, Diary.
27 MRC MSS 282/8/3/2, Diary consisting mainly of notes of discussions with Harold Wilson, 1963.

Some of his views were shattering. Talks of a wealth tax without understanding its implications or its extent. Assumes one cannot limit dividends or profits but can limit wages. Doesn't accept that NEDC should be a planning body with teeth [...] eventually recognises [...] that there will probably be a showdown on the wage restraint part of the discussion.[28]

Ultimately, in his reply to the debate itself, Callaghan repeated many of Cousins's key points about a 'planned growth of wages, not restraint'. Whether Callaghan did so spontaneously is unclear. The exchange underlined all the ambiguities that then existed around the ideas of public ownership and a 'planned economy'.[29]

Earlier at the 1963 TUC, Cousins had challenged his traditional ally, the TUC general secretary George Woodcock, when he argued for a measure of wage restraint if associated with agreed targets for economic growth as provided by the NEDC. Cousins's own speech to Congress made it clear that it was trade union members and not trade union leaders who counted in any dealings with government.

When I talk to the government about the London dockers, the country dockers, the country busmen, the factory workers and the road haulage workers they are much more influenced when I am saying the things that my members want me to say. We will not have wage restraint, whoever brings it and wraps it up for us.[30]

The only qualification to this position was made slightly earlier in the same speech when Cousins noted that 'when we have achieved a measure of planning and a Socialist government and, if I have to say to my members "We must now exercise restraint", I will say it and I will mean it'. Again it was not clear whether a socialist government was simply a Labour government and what a 'measure of planning' would be. Cousins's fight in 1960 was to ensure that the Labour Party held firm to its constitutional objectives: the full public ownership of the economy. The question was whether a Labour government, even if led by a previous defender of this radical constitution, was equipped to deliver it.

This is a question that returns us to our underlying theme of political transformation: how far had more radical left-wing perspectives developed within Britain's working-class movement by this stage? There was certainly a high level of unofficial strike action on the factory floor. There was also a broader range of occupations involved as active trade

28 MRC MSS 282/8/3/2, Diary.
29 MRC MSS 282/8/3/2, Diary.
30 Goodman, *Awkward Warrior*, p.367.

unionists, including scientific and technical workers, particularly those organised in TASS and ASTMS, and local government officers. 1961 had seen the first cross-industry, cross-union and all-British one-day wage strikes in the engineering and shipbuilding industries – with backing from the TGWU.[31] Elsewhere in the previously right-wing dominated engineering union, still largely the preserve of skilled workers, the Left had been making progress and the union would shortly see the election of Hugh Scanlon as general secretary.

Yet even within the TGWU there was still a quite entrenched right wing among some sections of the officers, with Harry Nicholas positioning himself as a potential leader. There were also, as noted previously, clear signs of support for right-wing attitudes on race. At the September 1963 TGWU GEC a motion from the historically radical and left-wing London bus workers to refuse to accept any more 'imported labour' was debated. This motion, passed at the Central Bus Conference, had also received broader backing from the Region 1 Passenger Services Group Committee. The motion condemned the 'use of deliberately imported labour' to jeopardise 'future negotiations to improve wages and conditions'. It was only with some difficulty that the executive managed to get the resolution withdrawn.[32]

31 MRC MSS 126/TG/1186/A/40, TGWU GEC minute for March 1962 gives the rationale for support for the strikes.
32 MRC MSS 126/TG/1186/A/41, TGWU GEC minute, 20 September 1963.

3

Labour in Government — but not Power

*In which Frank Cousins's hopes for socialist planning are thwarted
by Labour's alignment with the United States*

London's Royal Group of Docks

The Royal Group of Docks was developed along 250 acres of the Thames waterfront between East and West Ham from the 1850s to the 1920s. It was downstream from the main existing concentration of docks east of Tower Bridge and provided what was then the biggest and most modern and mechanised dock system in the world. The docks principally handled imports of food, especially frozen meat. At their peak they provided employment for around 10,000 dockers.

In the 1920s the London dockers had provided strong resistance to Bevin's centralised control of the union – directly confronting Bevin in the unofficial strike of 1923 – and were the base for an attempted breakaway Transport Union after the General Strike in 1926. The stevedores 'Blue Union' remained outside the TGWU throughout.

By the 1960s the Royal Group (the Royal Victoria, the Royal Albert and the King George V) was a stronghold of the unofficial liaison committee chaired by Jack Dash. It was this committee that produced the 1965 Dockers' Charter which, with its demand for nationalisation under workers' control, provided the rank-and-file challenge to the 1965 Devlin Report.[1] Four years later, in 1971–1972, the Royal Docks were one of the main centres of resistance to the use of containerisation aimed progressively at excluding

---

1 Final Report of the Committee of Inquiry Under the Rt. Hon. Lord Devlin into Certain Matters Concerning the Port Transport Industry (Her Majesty's Stationery Office, 1965).

the existing workforce of registered dockers from dock work. They picketed the new direct-load ship to rail depots being built further down the estuary and largely employing non-union labour. As this battle developed, the Royal Docks became the site of the climacteric confrontation between the trade union movement and the Tory government. As we will see, it was the imprisonment of the Pentonville Five, and the resulting strikes by dockers and subsequently workers from across Britain, which brought about the final defeat of the Industrial Relations Act in July–August 1972.

Jack Dash's 1969 autobiography gives a graphic description of the Royal Docks and of the style of work organisation that bred both solidarity and unofficial leadership – in some ways even more intensely than that in the motor industry. He takes us on the 6.15 a.m. bus to the main gates of the Royal Group. At 7.20 registered dock workers mass at the gates to examine the lists of shipping companies looking for labour (there were 34 different employers in the early 1960s, later reduced to ten). At 7.35 they pour through the gates and line up facing foremen of specific firms. At 7.45 precisely the foremen make their choices. The chosen dockers then move off in squads to specific ships. They examine and assess the cargoes in terms of how far piecework rates will pay them to shift it in the time required and whether more labour is needed. They then bargain with the foremen. If there is no agreement, the trade union official is called in, a dock area committee considers the issue and the recommendation is again put to the squad. If there is no agreement this may result in the declaration of an official dispute but generally not, and negotiations continue. At each stage it is the squad of workers that decides.[2]

This pattern of casualised employment had been imposed by the shipping employers. Faced with a constantly changing number of ships docking, each with differing labour requirements, they did not want to stand the costs of permanent labour forces. An end to casualisation had been discussed under the Labour governments of 1924 and 1929 and again repeatedly post-war. But little progress had been made. In terms of dockside industrial relations this system also had another important consequence. Because there was no permanent workforce for any employer, there were no officially elected shop stewards. While all workers were members of a union, mainly the TGWU but also some in the stevedores, it was in the daily process of wage bargaining that unofficial leaders developed who became the intermediaries with the paid trade union officials.

A survey of London dock workers in 1969–1970 found strong loyalty to Jack Dash's unofficial liaison committee and very strong support for solidarity action. When questioned 86 per cent backed strike action in the London docks to secure equal wages for those elsewhere in Britain. Politically, more than 80 per cent of dockers voted Labour – far above

2 Dash, *Good Morning, Brothers*, pp.98–100.

the average for industrial workers – and their politics were informed by a profile of Left values which included a strong opposition to all forms of social inequality. And they seem to have taken these positions in 1969 both because of, and despite, the struggles developing from the implementation of the Devlin Report by Labour between 1965 and 1970.[3]

In 1964 Lord Devlin, the same law lord who had earlier that year delivered the Rookes-Barnard judgement, was commissioned by the Wilson government to report on industrial relations in the docks. Devlin's remit was to recommend on how to develop more productive working practices and end the existing casualisation of dock labour. In his report Devlin directly attacked the TGWU for losing the 'confidence of the dockers' and thereby enabling Jack Dash's unofficial liaison committee to win support 'strong enough to amount to a rival power'. Devlin's strongest attack, however, was reserved for the liaison committee itself. He described its leaders as 'traitors in thought' and using the docks as 'a convenient battlefield on which to wage the class war'. He concluded: 'such men, whatever their motives, are wreckers'. His proposals to reduce the number of employers and create permanent workforces were in part designed to enable the election of 'official stewards' to displace the liaison committee. As we will see, this did not come about quite as Devlin had wished. But his appointment in November 1964, just after his Rookes-Barnard judgement, does raise questions about the political character of the Labour government which Frank Cousins joined as Minister of Technology in 1964.[4]

The First Wilson Government: What Role for Socialist Planning?

Harold Wilson was elected prime minister on 15 October 1964 as head of a Labour government with a majority of just three, shortly reduced to two after a by-election loss. Its election manifesto had promised:

A New Britain – mobilising the resources of technology under a national plan; harnessing our national wealth in brains, our genius for scientific invention and medical discovery; reversing the decline of the thirteen wasted years; affording a new opportunity to equal, and if possible surpass, the roaring progress of other western powers while Tory Britain has moved sideways, backwards but seldom forward.[5]

3 Stephen Hill, *The Dockers: Class and Tradition* (Heineman, 1976).

4 Devlin Report, pp.84–85; Michael Jackson, *Labour Relations in the Docks* (Saxon House, 1973); Michael Mellish, *Docks After Devlin* (Heineman, 1972).

5 '1964 Labour Party Election Manifesto: The New Britain', *Archive of Labour Party Manifestos*, paragraph 2, http://labour-party.org.uk/manifestos/1964/1964-labour-manifesto.shtml.

These objectives, it argued, will 'only be secured by a deliberate and massive effort to modernise the economy; to change its structure and to develop with all possible speed the advanced technology and the new science-based industries with which our future lies. In short, they will only be achieved by socialist planning'. What 'socialist planning' meant was left undefined. It involved a ministry of economic affairs that 'will frame broad strategy for increasing investment' and develop a 'national plan'. But the proposed role of the public sector was notably limited. Steel, which had been partly de-nationalised by the Tories, would be re-nationalised. Water, already partly nationalised, would be fully nationalised. Otherwise existing nationalised industries would be permitted to expand their commercial activities.

Additionally, a Ministry of Technology would be established to 'inject modern technology into our industries'. It would seek to extend the remit of government contracts for technology development from the military to civilian industry and go beyond research and development to establish 'new industries, either by public enterprise or in partnership with private industry'.[6]

It was as Minister of Technology that Frank Cousins entered Wilson's Cabinet in 1964. He had, as we have seen, earlier staked his union career on defending the Labour Party's Clause 4 and the commitment to comprehensive public ownership. In the debates of 1963–1964 he had argued for 'planning with teeth', a phrase that Wilson himself had adopted. Now it remained to be seen how far this commitment would go.

At the outset the Cabinet was divided between a largely dominant right wing led by George Brown, James Callaghan and Michael Stewart and a 'moderate' left-wing, centrists who wanted policies less dependent on the US, led by Crossman and Barbara Castle. The left wing was advised by the economists Kaldor and Balogh, not socialists but left-Keynesians with a commitment to growth and active industrial planning. The policy advisers of the right wing were largely the Nuffield industrial relations experts led by Allan Flanders who had been key allies of Gaitskell. The right wing soon established its dominance and ensured that all the key levers of economic policy were concentrated in the hands of either George Brown at the Department of Economic Affairs (DEA) or James Callaghan at the Treasury. Cousins was left with little more than an advisory role in a government that quickly surrendered any plans for state-led industrial investment. Within a matter of weeks it had reverted to policies very similar to those of its Tory predecessor, suppressing wage growth in the hope of encouraging private investment.[7]

These developments largely vindicated Cousins's own understanding of the power dynamics of the Labour Party as demonstrated back in 1960. As

6 '1964 Labour Party Election Manifesto: The New Britain'.
7 Middlemas, *Power, Competition and the State: Threats*, pp.115–117.

we noted earlier, Cousins saw any significant move towards socialist public ownership as closely dependent on how far Labour ended its economic and military alignment with the US. Immediately after the election there was a short-lived bid for independence. Castle and Crossman, backed by Balogh and Kaldor, urged devaluation as the only way to boost exports and give the government leeway for expansionist policies. This proposal was quickly blocked by Brown and Callaghan with the explicit backing of the US government and its financial institutions. At the time the escalation of the Vietnam war was placing heavy pressure on the dollar's grossly overvalued link to gold at $35 an ounce. Any devaluation by Britain would intensify this pressure. The US position was therefore emphatic. The pound must not be devalued. US support was conditional on solving the problem in a quite different way – by cutting imports and boosting exports. And this meant controlling consumption and wages.[8]

Between November 1964 and July 1965 the US intervened three times. This first intervention, immediately after the election in November, was followed by a detailed oversight of the preparation of Jim Callaghan's budget in March–April 1965. A leading state department official was sent over to work with the Treasury – again cutting government expenditure and increasing taxes. Then in the summer of 1965 there was a new sterling crisis. This time the price of support for the pound was a formal pact negotiated between Wilson and President Johnson.[9] In return for further loans it required the maintenance of existing levels of British support for NATO, a continuing military presence East of Suez, diplomatic support for the US presence in Vietnam and a progressive reduction in Britain's external deficit through cuts in imports and domestic consumption. At the time only a very limited number of Cabinet colleagues were aware of the full nature and character of this pact or indeed that any formal agreement had been concluded. Cousins, for one, would not have known about it. He would, however, have known of the pressures from the IMF and Washington not to devalue and to cut expenditure.

Wilson's own position is not clear. He may have been an unwilling prisoner of the right wing. He certainly made efforts to moderate US policy in Vietnam. In the spring of 1965, after facing backbench pressure over the

8 These assessments are based on Goodman, *Awkward Warrior*, chapter 21; and Middlemas, *Power, Competition and the State: Threats*, chapter 4.

9 The full scale of the backstairs negotiations with the United States, and the subsequent supervision, has only been documented comparatively recently. The role of the state department official in April 1965 was kept a close secret at the time: TNA PREM 13/678, Foreign Office-Washington, 4 April 1965; Jonathan Coleman, *A Special Relationship: Harold Wilson, Lyndon Johnson and Angle-American Relations 1964–68* (Manchester University Press, 2018), footnotes 49–51; Kevin Boyle, 'The Price of Peace, Vietnam, the Pound and the Close of the American Empire', *Diplomatic History*, 2003, vol.27, no.1, pp.37–72.

US use of blanket bombing, napalm and poison gas, he even went as far as involving the Soviet prime minister Kosygin in a potential peace conference only to be rebuffed by Johnson.[10] But in terms of domestic policy and pledges on state intervention, he had already capitulated to Brown and Callaghan. On 13 November 1964 Frank Soskice, the attorney general, presented the Cabinet with a paper, supported by the right-wing Minister of Labour Ray Gunter, authorising the declaration of a state of emergency and the use of 30,000 troops to break a threatened dock strike – and it was at this point that Lord Devlin was appointed to investigate industrial relations in the docks.[11]

Frank Cousins was left to organise his own department, and even find his own office, with no support, and significant interference, from George Brown at the DEA. Cousin's two key advisers were Patrick Blackett FRS, one of Britain's most distinguished scientists, and Lord Penny who had previously worked on Britain's own nuclear weapons.[12] Lord Kearton, of ICI, chaired a new advisory council of industrialists. C.P. Snow, the Oxford-based scientist and novelist, became his parliamentary secretary.

By November 1965 Cousins had established working parties to advise on policy for four key industries considered to be 'lagging' internationally: machine tools, electronics, telecoms and computers. Any government financial aid would require government oversight to ensure that investment was actually made and made wisely. This did result in an important initiative to rescue Britain's computer industry and also to salvage research and development on civil nuclear energy at Dounreay. However, the wider plans failed. There was no money to give and no significant intervention took place. Cousin's subsequent proposal to create an industrial reorganisation corporation was seized by George Brown and transferred to the DEA.

At the same time the Labour government's moves towards a statutory, enforceable incomes policy were hardening – despite TGWU opposition at the 1965 TUC. Brown had established a Prices and Incomes Board in December 1964, demanded action on wage inflation in June 1965 and finally in November 1965 called for statutory powers to enforce an incomes policy.[13]

By then Cousins was actively considering his position. He was dismayed at the direction of the government, its subordination to US

10 Jonathan Coleman, *A Special Relationship*, citing TNA PREM 13/678, 4 April 1965.

11 TNA CAB 129 119/15, Soskice to Cabinet, 13 November 1964.

12 Goodman, *Awkward Warrior*, chapter 22, documents Cousins's problems in securing any wider support within the Cabinet. Blackett was even denied access to routine policy papers because his opposition to nuclear weapons was deemed to make him a security risk.

13 Middlemas, *Power, Competition and the State: Threats*, pp.135–138.

policy, particularly in Vietnam, and the consequent enforcement of wage restraint and the threats to trade union freedom. But he was also concerned at developments in the TGWU itself. In 1963 he had brought Jack Jones into Transport House as assistant general secretary, to strengthen the implementation of policy in his absence. But the acting general secretary was Harry Nicholas, an officer from the Deakin era. Although publicly loyal and committed to existing union policy, he was politically much closer to George Brown, himself an ex-TGWU officer and TGWU-sponsored member of parliament (MP). Key area and trade group secretaries from the previous era also looked for a shift of political direction and were acutely uncomfortable with the unleashing of member democracy by Cousins and Jones. By the end of 1965 John Cousins, now a TGWU official, was warning his father of the critical internal position in the union. If Cousins remained in the government, Nicholas would succeed as general secretary, Jack Jones would be excluded and the union would very probably swing back to the right. Ahead of the imminent general election, Frank Cousins stayed his hand. He wanted no damage to the government. But by early 1966 he had determined to resign once the election was over.[14]

The Battle to Defend Wages and Trade Union Rights Continues

Throughout the term of the 1964–1966 Labour government inflation was running high – up from 3.3 per cent in 1964 to 4.8 in 1965. George Brown sought to secure public sector wage limits of 2.5 per cent in 1964. By 1965 he wanted statutory powers to enforce a 3.5 per cent limit.

The dockers were the most consistent opponents of what they correctly saw as attempts to erode their real wages. Already in the early 1960s the unofficial liaison committee, mainly based in the London docks but also with significant backing in Hull and Liverpool, was mobilising support that successfully resisted attempts by the docks trade group national secretary Tim O'Leary to hold back unofficial action. In June 1960 O'Leary had to concede the replacement of officers in Liverpool by Jack Jones and moves to incorporate hitherto unofficial leaders in an attempt to halt the formation of an independent local union.[15] In October O'Leary was calling for local action by officials to counter agitation against the wage settlement negotiated that summer, particularly in London and Liverpool.[16] He commented 'given a few loyal and courageous men in each port' these

---

14 Goodman, *Awkward Warrior*, chapter 23, gives the personal account from Cousins and his family.

15 MRC MSS 126/TG/ 439/1/18, TGWU Docks Group minutes, 1960–61, 1 June 1960.

16 MRC MSS 126/TG/ 439/1/18, TGWU Docks Group minutes, 17 August 1960.

attempts could be 'smashed'. The minute of 7 March 1961 notes further 'steps to counter unofficial action'. Through 1961 and 1962 momentum was gathering for national strike action for a significant wage increase. The National Delegate Conference on 27 April 1962 saw O'Leary's calls for postponement heavily defeated. The threat of strike action on 14 May was sufficient to win a major advance in wages. The July meeting of the union's executive council congratulated the dock's group on the 'splendid result' and noted its significance for other claims.[17]

In July 1964 an unofficial one-day strike took place in Hull, London and Merseyside to demand a wage increase that would compensate for the 7 per cent inflation since 1962. It was repeated in October as the new Labour government took office. It was the subsequent threat of a national strike that saw the incoming Labour government make arrangements for a state of emergency, the calling in of Devlin and then the offer of a significant advance that was accepted in November 1964 pending the outcome of Devlin's enquiry.

The report was published in August 1965. It was seen by O'Leary and his officers as a major opportunity to seize back control – and, of course, this was very much the intention of Devlin himself. The meeting of the Docks Group on 17 August 1965 made preparations for winning support for the proposals on almost military lines.[18] It was announced that the union had purchased several sets of 'very powerful' loudspeaker equipment. Officers were allocated to particular docks. Schedules were compiled for dock gate meetings. Copies of the report were to be distributed together with a special broadsheet produced by the TGWU. The objective was to secure 'a virile and active lay membership who would support officers' ahead of the creation of 'a full and effective shops steward system' once new employment structures had been created. The broadsheet clearly defined 'the enemy': 'those who refuse to take part in this – who refuse to support the union and take part in the democratic decision are [...] the enemies of their fellow workers'.[19]

By the October meeting of the Docks Group it was clear that these arrangements were not going according to plan. The new wage settlement promised by Devlin had been delayed. Official dock meetings had been postponed. Instead the liaison committee was holding meetings around the Dockers Charter – posing public ownership against the maintenance of a consolidated system of private employers. The scale of the meeting held in the West India Dock was seen as particularly alarming – being outside the liaison committee's traditional stronghold of the Royals. One

17 MRC MSS 126/TG.439/1/19, 12 January 1962, 19 April 1962, 27 March 1962, 27 April 1962 (Delegate Conference); Docks National Committee, 16 May 1962.

18 MRC MSS 126/TG/447/33/1, Special Meeting Docks Group Committee, 17 August 1965.

19 As reproduced in the TGWU *Record* for October 1965.

officer complained 'we are losing ground fast'.[20] The meeting decided to 'summon' 'Bros Barratt, Cole and Dash' to the next meeting. This seems to have been a serious tactical mistake. On 26 November they were subjected to a very long lecture by Jack Dash on the merits of the Dockers Charter – and the following day found the *Sun* newspaper, previously the *Daily Herald* and not at that time owned by Rupert Murdoch, reporting that the Docks Group committee had accepted the liaison committee's ten points.[21]

Hence, still in the spring of 1966 the authority of the liaison committee remained unchallenged and by May of that year, as Wilson was assembling his new post-election Cabinet, dockers in London, Liverpool and Hull were beginning to take unofficial action in support of the seafarers' first official strike for half a century.[22] This act of solidarity caused consternation in the Cabinet but also underlined the progressive politics of the dockers. As unofficial strikers they were putting their own livelihood (and possibly jobs) on the line – but they also knew that their action was critical for the success of the seafarers' struggle. The docks had to be stopped if all ships, foreign as well as British, were to be brought to a standstill. Wilson, well briefed by the security services, then made his extraordinary attack in the Commons on the seafarers' leaders. By then it was clear that the second Wilson government would continue down the same road as the first. There would be no socialist planning.

Advancing from the 'Fortresses of the Working Class': The Balance Sheet for 1960 to 1966

Section I has examined three of the 'fortresses' of the British working class: Longbridge, Heathrow and the London docks. All demonstrate how, in different ways, working-class strength was developed over previous decades and then consolidated in the first half of the 1960s.

At Longbridge these developments were not easy and took a long time. The way work had originally been organised in this giant factory in the 1920s was designed to control labour and eliminate the power that had been exercised by the skilled engineering unions up to the end of the First World War. Car components were to be assembled by non-skilled workers and the speed of the assembly line was to give management control over output and productivity. For almost a generation, as we noted, Longbridge remained a non-union plant – apart from very small pockets of skilled craftsmen. But full employment during the Second World War

20 MRC MSS 126/TG/447/33/1, Docks Group Committee, 6 October 1965.
21 MRC MSS 126/TG/439/1/20, Docks Group Committee, 26 November 1965 and 29 November 1965.
22 MRC MSS 126/TG/439/1/20, Docks Group Committee, 20 and 31 May 1965.

and thereafter, and, crucially, the detailed organisational work of union activists like Dick Etheridge, turned the previous weakness on its head. The assembly line enabled any group of workers to halt output. It gave immediate power to shop stewards representing workers in the workplace as against externally-based trade union officers. And within the workplace it also demanded the development of a unity that went beyond particular departments or unions.

This was the position as it developed through the 1950s. What happened then? As we have seen, from about 1958 the Conservative government sought to transform industrial development in the face of much faster industrial growth in Germany, Japan and France. Critically and predictably, the necessary investment was to be secured on terms set by big business and at labour's expense. New plants were to be established in areas of higher unemployment in the north and west. Labour was to be shed from coal and rails. Unemployment was to be allowed to rise a little everywhere. At the same time, whether by design or accident, higher levels of inflation reduced real wages as big monopoly producers increased prices. And as workers sought to defend their living standards the government sought to limit wage increases – first in areas where it was a major employer, like Heathrow and the docks, and then generally.

These years did see important new developments in trade union organisation. From 1960 the TGWU was bringing together workers on a company basis from the new plants on Merseyside, Scotland and South Wales along with those in the Midlands and the South East. Joint shop stewards committees at company level were being formed. At the same time, at 'Confed' level, united cross-union industrial action was being organised. 1962 saw the first all-Britain one-day strikes on wages across the engineering industry. In this way a new national trade union unity was being formed – particularly at shop steward level. However, it was a unity that was essentially defensive. It protected wages and living standards. But it could not change policy.

The question was, how could workers move forward from their newly created workplace fortresses and effect the fundamental economic and social change that was required?

It was for this reason that trade union strategists like Frank Cousins saw the Labour Party as so important. It was the party of organised labour. It was based in the trade union movement. Its constitution committed it to the social ownership of the means of production. It therefore offered the possibility of a quite different path for industrial modernisation, one in which socialist planning ensured that investment was made, that the power of the big monopoly producers was challenged and that the state itself organised the transformation of industry and did so in a way that strengthened and did not weaken organised labour.

As we have seen, Cousins very clearly understood the limitations of the Labour Party. He saw the fight to defend the party's socialist objectives as closely linked to the fight against nuclear weapons and the US alliance. Britain's dependence on the US was not just dangerous and immoral. It made Britain an economic hostage. Worse than this, as we have seen, the Labour Party under Hugh Gaitskell, and largely thereafter, was run by people committed to a US world view both organisationally and financially. It was this dominance that Cousins sought to break. His objective was to revive the pro-socialist forces previously grouped round Aneurin Bevan. As we have seen, his initial victory was only limited and temporary. The real challenge, as Cousins put it, was to transform 'the many millions of trade union members' from being 'socialists in embryo' into 'conscious socialists'.

This need was demonstrated only too well by the Labour government that took office in 1964. The government was trapped not so much by its financial dependence on the US but because a majority of its leadership supported that relationship and rejected the clear and obvious alternative of devaluing the pound. Section II will examine the sequel. Over the four years to 1970 the Wilson government moved from voluntary incomes policies to threatening imprisonment – without any move towards the wider social ownership of industry. Politically, Labour's failure to deliver economic advance and social renewal brought disillusion and in some cases a resurgence of right-wing, divisive and racist views.

Overall, however, movement was in the other direction. The TGWU was joined by the AEU under Hugh Scanlon in a new radical alliance. The shop stewards movement developed a level of national organisation, and scale of mass mobilisation, that enabled it to challenge and defeat the attack on trade union power. The process of wider political transformation was underway.

Southampton Docks and Containerisation

John Fisher

The introduction of decasualisation and modernisation in the port transport industry – commonly known as the Devlin agreements – was the biggest change in the industry since the Dock Labour Scheme in 1947 and set the pattern for the industry which is still with us today. The negotiations took more than a decade and led to huge conflicts and disruption, yet it was said at the time that '[i]n Southampton, modernisation has proved itself, in London it has been a disaster [...]. It gives a textbook example of new co-operation, not conflict' (D.F. Wilson, 'Port Modernisation Proves Itself in Southampton', *Financial Times*, 13 April 1971). Yet Southampton was a fully unionised port, with only one union – the T&G. It was well organised, with an established system of shop stewards. So how did the changes come about without the conflict seen in other major ports?

The key thing to realise about Southampton is that it had, and has, a very fortunate location. It is the only major cargo port on the south coast; the other ports – Plymouth, Poole, Portsmouth and Dover – are either military or mainly cross-channel facilities. It has good rail and now road links to London and the Midlands, and four high tides every 24 hours and a deep and sheltered harbour. The balance of cargo coming through the port has always been favourable, even in periods of economic depression. A total of 90 per cent of South Africa's fruit trade came through Southampton, and even in 1938 the port handled 560,000 passengers on the great Cunard and White Star liners. In that year it still handled 19 million tons of freight (the figure for 2018 was 34 million tons). As the rise of civil air transport ended the age of transatlantic liners, the burgeoning holiday cruising industry made Southampton its base. As general cargo was overtaken by containerisation, the tidal advantage and location allowed ships to have a rapid turnaround, and Southampton became a major container port and the UK number one port for car imports and exports. After the war, London dockers who had worked at the military port at Marchwood, attempted to introduce the 'Blue' stevedores' union into Southampton, but this was rejected as representing the 'blue-eyed boys' of the London casual system (Jack Dash, *Good Morning, Brothers* (Mayflower, 1969) pp.82–83).

Not only that. For a medium-sized city, Southampton was blessed with employment opportunities, mainly for men, both skilled and unskilled. In the post-war period there were large centres of employment in Ford, Pirelli, Vosper-Thorneycroft, British American Tobacco (BAT), Rank, Phillips Electrical, and just outside the city the huge Fawley oil and chemicals complex and Eastleigh Railway Works. Pirelli, Ford, Eastleigh Railway Works, BAT and Rank have now gone or been reduced to depots, yet up to the 2020 pandemic, unemployment in Southampton was still very low, at around 4 per cent. Southampton dockers were not therefore operating like their brothers in Hull or Liverpool, surrounded by a low-wage, high unemployment economy. All these named companies were also unionised, with the T&G playing a major role. They were not sweatshops, but often provided well-paid jobs with good conditions, so did not undermine the dockers' situation, as in some other ports.

There was only the T&G, but there were some special features; Southampton struck in 1890, following their brothers in London, but were not supported by the London-based leadership of the dockers' union, and from that time they became insular. Their situation of relative prosperity and security resulted in the establishment of a union organisation much more similar to an established factory than the casualism of London or Glasgow. (It is worth recalling that in 1947 the Glasgow dockers opposed the National Dock Labour Board (NDLB) system of registration and maintenance as they preferred to be casual and 'free'.) The result was that in Southampton there were established shop stewards and an established, even cozy, relationship between the employers and the union leadership, especially with Ernie Allen, the T&G regional secretary. Ernie Allen was one of the key drivers of the famous Fawley productivity deal in 1960. He saw this as a way forward for workers in a competitive world. Allen would have seen the Devlin negotiations as a huge example of a productivity deal. However, many on the left saw this as a sell-out and a way of increasing the exploitation of workers for little in return (for both sides see Alan Flanders, *The Fawley Productivity Agreements* (Faber, 1964); Tony Cliff, *The Employers' Offensive: Productivity Deals and How to Fight Them* (Pluto Press, 1970)).

However, it was the shop stewards who negotiated the decasualisation and modernisation agreements in Southampton, not more distant full-time officials. This was to be a key element in the fact that the agreements came in without a strike. Southampton was the only port to be represented on the National Modernisation Committee by a shop steward rather than a full-time official. The chair and secretary of the shop stewards' committee and members of the Local Modernisation Committee, Bill Whitlock and Dennis Harryman, were aware of the criticisms of productivity deals and kept a close eye on Ernie Allen. Nothing was agreed in Southampton without the approval of the shop stewards. Bill Whitlock had good leadership qualities and was trusted by the men. Dennis Harryman was the 'brains'. He later became T&G docks officer, regional organiser, councillor and mayor of Southampton.

Containerisation meant that port transport could change from a labour-intensive to a mechanised, semi-automated state, as cargoes of all shapes and sizes were shipped in standardised 40 (or 20) feet x 8 feet boxes. The McKinsey Report of 1967 predicted that this would mean that 90 per cent of dockers would lose their jobs (McKinsey and Co. Inc., *Containerisation: The Key to Low-Cost Transport* (British Transport Docks Board, 1967)). The union leadership (especially the national officer, Tim O'Leary) took the view that this could not be opposed, but that in return for acceptance of the principle, and for (almost) 24-hour coverage, there should be job security for those remaining after redundancy, and an acceptable basic wage. Mainly it was seen by the union leadership as a real chance to end casual labour, something they had campaigned against for almost a century. Without fundamentally challenging the ownership and control of the industry, the union felt it was difficult to oppose the re-structuring of the industry. Only Liverpool challenged this view. At a time when the arguments about money involved a figure of £35–£38 per week for 40 hours, the Liverpool dockers put forward a policy of £60 for 20 hours. This was for too radical for the union, and indeed for Southampton.

The context for these negotiations were the Devlin Reports of 1965 and 1966, which set out the overall strategy for decasualisation and modernisation (*Final Report of the Committee of Inquiry under the Rt. Hon. Lord Devlin into Certain Matters Concerning the Port Transport Industry,* GB Ministry of Labour, HMSO, 1965; *Report of the Committee of Inquiry under Lord Devlin into the Wages Structure and Level of Pay for Dock Workers, Etc.,* GB Ministry of Labour, HMSO, 1966). The employers' demands were as follows:

1. Redundancy, through voluntary severance and 'natural wastage'

2. The end of 'Restrictive Practices'. This was to be a major conflict issue

3. Turnaround time and shift working

4. The abolition of piecework

5. Permanent employment.

In Southampton, the negotiations were partly driven by strategic developments in the port. Southampton was singled out as an ideal port for container traffic, and large investments were made long before the final Devlin agreements. The container terminal opened in stages from 1968 and the employers were vulnerable to a ban on working containers. However, the relatively small number of dockers (1,700) meant that the employers were willing to be flexible on pay, so long as they could get as near to round-the-clock working as possible. The age-profile of dockers showed the great majority to be between 40 and 64 years of age, so the employers knew that many would take redundancy if offered. Southampton was ideally situated for fast turnaround, and Southampton dockers had been more-or-less permanently employed under the Dock Labour Scheme. The employers also agreed to reduce the number of employers from five to one. The union nationally claimed that it was the myriad of small employers in the ports who wanted to hang onto piecework, and the union supported the idea of a few large employers, particularly nationalised ones like the British Transport Docks Board, as they would be the basis of permanent employment with good wages and conditions. The new single employer, Southampton Cargo Handling Company (a merger of the British Transport Docks Board and South Coast Stevedores) came into being on 1 January 1968. The port was taken over by Associated British Ports (ABP) in 2006 following the privatisation of the BTDB under Thatcher and the purchase of the company by Goldman-Sachs. The sticky issue of 'mobility' was fairly easily resolved in Southampton as since the war it had been a tradition for the shop stewards to manage the allocation of work and transfers, so, unlike ports like London, there were no 'perms' and 'casuals', no 'gangs' and much more fairness. It was agreed that the shop stewards should continue in this role, and manning levels remained about the same. There was a temporary register, but this was often treated as an informal 'apprenticeship' as it was normal for 'temps' to become fully registered dockers. The union wanted to turn this register into a formal apprenticeship scheme.

On pay, a national agreement was reached in September 1967 giving a minimum daily wage of 44s 4d (£2.22) for eight hours; a modernisation payment of 1s (5p) per hour; a guarantee of £15 per week for five days. In Southampton this was improved with a 10s (50p) per week mobility payment, and only 'reasonable mobility' could be demanded, with the maintenance of manning scales and the fair transfer system.

Now began the negotiations for Phase 2: modernisation. In June 1968 the shop stewards issued the Southampton Dockers' Charter. This document called for a four-day week of 35 hours, along with other benefits like sick pay and holidays, but also accepted 24-hour, seven-day working. The target wage was set at £40. After much argument and the breakdown of negotiations, including Southampton's involvement in the national dock strike in July 1970, an agreement was finally reached in September 1970 on this basis:

1. Two shifts per day; Monday–Friday 8am to 5pm and 5pm to midnight

2. 24-hour working on specialised berths: maintenance of the roster allocation system

3. £38 10s (£38 50p) for 40 hours

4. Complete flexibility, but some concessions (e.g. Sunday working)

5. Sick pay and improved training.

This agreement was signed on 27 November 1970. There was opposition, mainly around the abandonment of the £40 target and the 35-hour week, and some felt that the union could have achieved a better deal. However, many understood that with allowances associated with round-the-clock working, real take-home pay would be much higher than the basic. For their part, the employers threatened to move their trade to Tilbury or Felixstowe, but no one took this too seriously.

Local bargaining meant that the shop stewards maintained ownership of this agreement. Generally they were in harmony with their local officials but more suspicious of employers. On the other hand, they put the interests of 'their' port above all else. The idea of 'orbits of coercive comparison' seems quite relevant here (See A.M. Ross, *Trade Union Wage Policy,* University of California, 1948. The point is that particular groups of workers have other identified groups with whom they compare themselves and make demands based on these particular groups rather than others. In Southampton's case it was London). To Southampton dockers, no one else mattered except London. This was the port which they compared themselves to and wanted to match. But it was a double-edged sword. This was also the port that the dockers wanted to undercut to protect themselves and their future employment. In this sense, the agreements reached on the National Modernisation Committee were seen as a basis to improve upon, but only so far as it did not make Southampton vulnerable. They were fortunate that geographical factors and decisions to expand Southampton as a future container port worked in their favour, as did the tradition of fairness developed over the years through the shop stewards and only having one union in the port. The union's demands in Southampton were clear, but limited in scope. They accepted the principle of productivity bargaining and never made demands for the nationalisation of the industry or democratic management of the industry. They accepted the competitive ethic for their port. On reflection, it is clear that the way Southampton operated under the Dock Labour Scheme was nearly in line with the Devlin proposals; there was only one union and only five employers, and there were shop stewards who controlled and limited much of the unfairness of casual employment in ports like London. Under this system there was much flexibility and in practice almost full employment.

For their part, the employers accepted that Southampton was a 'golden nugget' for their profitability, and did not attempt to undermine Devlin by building depots outside the port using non-registered labour, as happened in London. Once again, Southampton's favoured situation allowed those who might have become registered dockers to find employment in the many industries associated with the continuing expansion of the port. Today the port supports around 15,000 jobs and handles more trade for countries outside the European Union than any other UK port. Like much else, it is now privatised, and the union still has much to do within a basically successful and favoured port (for the full details of decasualisation and modernisation in Southampton, see the unpublished PhD thesis held by the University of Southampton: J.P. Fisher, 'The TGWU and the Devlin Modernisation Programme in the Port Transport Industry, with Particular Reference to Southampton' (University of Southampton, 1976)).

Dr John Fisher developed trade union education programmes mainly with the TGWU as a lecturer at Surrey University from the 1970s, and in 1996 became Director of Research and Education for the union. He retired in 2007.

Some Issues for Discussion

1. How important was the role of the TGWU's leadership in driving the development of a shop stewards movement in this period? Would it have developed anyway?

2. What was the wider political significance of the TGWU's opposition to Britain's nuclear bomb?

3. Was Frank Cousins correct in his decision to enter the 1964 Labour government, and what lessons can be drawn?

4. How important was discussion and debate in and around the workplace for the development of a politically more engaged membership, and did this 'politicisation' create new divisions or help to overcome them?

5. In terms of asserting the interests of dockers in improving their conditions and preserving their jobs, what were the relative merits of the approach of the dockers liaison committee and that adopted in Southampton?

II

1966–1970

The Forward March of the Labour Party Halted: The TGWU Marches On

This section documents Frank Cousins's return to the union, the election of Jack Jones as his successor and their joint drive to democratise the union and develop lay member power. It details the battles by black members to overcome embedded discrimination and the equal pay challenge by women members at Ford. It concludes by documenting the TGWU's role in defeating the Wilson government's attempt to impose penal sanctions on shop stewards. Its two case studies examine road transport in the Midlands and the Ford plant at Dagenham.

4

Facing a Right-wing Labour Government

In which Frank Cousins and Jack Jones hold the union on a
leftward course despite difficult challenges

From the Driver's Cab

Throughout the 1960s shop stewards of the Midlands 5/35 Road Transport branch met monthly in the AEU's Grand Hall in Central Birmingham. They met there because the TGWU had no hall big enough to accommodate the average attendance of 350 stewards. It was also a very appropriate setting. The brutalist 1950s glass and concrete building well matched the tactics of the branch and its full-time officer, Allan Law.

Law had been appointed as full-time officer for the branch in 1958 by the then Region 5 secretary Jack Jones. Law, an ex-paratrooper, believed, like Jones, in the importance of member-led action. Over the following decade he, together with his branch members, transformed the status of road transport drivers in the Midlands, increased branch membership from 2,000 to over 5,000 and secured a differential rate of pay for the Midlands over all other regions of the union. Just before his retirement he wrote: 'the strength of the workers rests solely with the workers themselves. No amount of laws, rules and regulations can do any good unless the people are prepared to get up and organise'.[1]

Commercial road transport had traditionally been very difficult to organise. Frank Cousins himself had started his TGWU working life as

---

1 Tony Corfield, *The Rule of Law: A Study in Trade Union Organisation and Method* (Brierley Publications, 1982), p.99. The following account is largely drawn from this study and also from Paul Smith's *Unionisation and Union Leadership* (Routledge, 2001).

a commercial driver in the 1930s before moving on to become a union organiser for the sector. The post-war nationalisation of the big operators had proved short-lived – although British Road Services (BRS), the biggest employer, did survive under public ownership through the 1960s. Most drivers in the 1950s were employed by small regional firms with less than 50 lorries and many with just two or three. The result was an occupation with low wages, poor working conditions and little union leverage. Collective agreements and full unionisation was restricted to BRS and a limited number of large firms – generally managed and policed by full-time union officers.

Law and the 5/35 branch broke this mould. The main tactic was to pick on a company with highly vulnerable delivery schedules, win compliance on improved wages and conditions and then use this to pressurise other companies – along the way recruiting drivers and broadening the base of the branch. Each regulatory change by government – increases in permitted speeds, the attempted introduction of the tachograph – would be used to leverage new concessions.

The key turning point came with two disputes in 1965–1966. Law used leverage over one relatively large company in the Millichamp dispute to win a settlement across the Birmingham area 'hire and reward' (commercial contracting) sector that secured a 13.5 per cent increase, broke the Labour government's incomes policy and established a differential that put the Midlands ahead of other regions. The second dispute was in support of drivers on BMC Longbridge car transporters. Again Law attacked vulnerable supply lines together with the leverage supplied by a settlement with a Coventry employer. The resulting lay-offs at BMC plants brought a government enquiry and an outcome which achieved Law's objective: putting drivers' wage levels near those of skilled workers in engineering – an outcome, as Harry Urwin pointed out, that was all the more remarkable because it was achieved during a period of serious depression in the car industry.[2] By 1969 the branch had succeeded in enforcing a pre-entry union closed shop across the Birmingham area's commercial contracting sector. A union card check was required before any driver could start work.[3]

Law's tactics won him the loyalty of the rapidly expanding 5/35 branch membership – as well as that of the other commercial transport branches in the Midlands. But they also created very considerable tensions with the officers of the National Road Transport (Commercial) Group as well as with some other regions. The minutes of the National Road Transport

2 J. Scamp, Longbridge Delivery Agents, Command 2905, 18 February 1966, Parliamentary Papers (available in most major libraries); Harry Urwin, TGWU *Record*, February 1967.

3 Smith, *Unionisation*, p.125.

(Commercial) Committee for the mid-1960s show constant battles. Law accused the national secretary A.G. Beck of negotiating agreements at national level without consultation – arguing they were detrimental to the Midlands. Beck accused Law of negotiating regional agreements that broke and threatened to overturn national agreements – and in this complaint was supported by other regions, principally the biggest, London and South East, that were much more dependent on officer-led negotiation.[4]

These conflicts exposed very different regional circumstances. London was still dominated by officers from the Deakin era. It was also far more dependent on traditional industries, the docks and the wholesale food markets, and was by the 1960s beginning to see large-scale industry migrating elsewhere. Membership was stagnant and in 1966 actually declined. Merseyside again was different. At the beginning of the 1960s it had a legacy of Deakin era officers still policing the docks and the region as a whole, which nonetheless maintained an underlying tradition of radical militancy. The arrival of new large-scale industrial plants on Merseyside in the 1960s – motors, glass, rubber – provided the basis for a transformation of organisation and political direction both generally and in road transport. By the late sixties, when Merseyside was merged into a larger North West region, it was Liverpool and Birkenhead that was the more radical and left wing.[5]

These regional differences resulted in differing responses to the biggest challenge of the late sixties and early seventies: containerisation. It also generated somewhat different types of union politics. Although appointed by Jack Jones and carrying forward his commitment to member-led trade unionism, Law did not share Jones's wider socialist perspectives or his strategic vision of moving beyond limited trade-identified perspectives and creating a new trade union, or even class solidarity. For Law and his members, loyalty was focused on their trade. The otherwise isolated and exploited individual driver found a new collective loyalty among fellow road haulage workers. The drive for 100 per cent trade unionism, and a militant disregard for national procedures, also saw Law successfully lead a consortium of regional TGWU branches to impose union rates and conditions on the new Birmingham container base in 1969.

The process in London was far more fraught and conflictual. London carried forward its own radical current but one largely locked within very strong traditional trade identities in which locality and often family played a major part, especially in the docks and the great wholesale markets such as

4 MRC MSS 126/TG/676/1/5, National Road Transport (Commercial) Group Committee minutes for 21 October 1965. This dispute continued on 21 April 1966.

5 This assessment and that in the following paragraphs is largely based on Paul Smith's very insightful examination in *Unionisation* of union development in different regions.

Smithfield and Covent Garden. In the unofficial haulage strikes in the early sixties, bonds of local solidarity between drivers and dockers and market porters were important in defending conditions for both drivers and market workers. Yet in the later 1960s and early 1970s containerisation brought open conflict between the dockers' JSSC and road transport workers and TGWU General Workers section over the control of the new container depots at Tilbury and Dagenham. In July 1972 the dockers unofficial liaison committee placed pickets on the new depots to demand the removal of their fellow TGWU members. Although this antagonism immediately dissolved in face of government action to arrest and imprison the pickets, sectional loyalty remained a potential source of conflict as well as strength.

Overall, however, the trend was not towards trade sectionalism. The period into the 1970s saw significantly higher levels of unionisation among haulage workers, the development of wider trade union identities and – in the face of first Labour and then Conservative attacks – a determination to defend existing trade union freedoms. For the miners in 1972 and again 1974 the strength of unionisation among commercial drivers, and their wider trade union loyalty, was to prove crucial in halting the movement of coal and ensuring the defeat of the Conservative government.

'The Great Tradition of Independent Working-Class Power'

Frank Cousins returned to his post as general secretary in autumn 1966 once the general election was over. As we have seen, he did so partly to pre-empt increasingly active attempts by regional and trade group officers, tacitly supported by the acting general secretary Harry Nicholas, to change the union's direction. More critically, however, it was because Cousins believed that it was now the union that – politically – offered the way forward. The Labour government was locked into policies that committed it to conformity with the needs of big business and in consequence to attacking basic trade union rights. In these circumstances the role of the TGWU would be critical. It had the capability to develop alliances within the trade union movement that could resist these attacks and, no less important, in the course of doing so it had the potential to re-win a mass understanding among working people of what was needed to secure the socialist objectives that Cousins had advanced at the Labour Party conferences of 1960 and 1961.

In the TGWU *Record* for January 1967, Cousins launched a sharp attack on the government's handling of the economy. Its drastic deflation had caused 'the biggest drop in output since the 1962–63 crisis'.[6] It had attacked workers instead of tackling the real cause of the balance of

6 TGWU *Record*, January 1967.

payments crisis: the 'vast sums' wasted on overseas military expenditure. Wages in Britain, he pointed out, were lower than those elsewhere in Europe and attempts to 'take away the right of workers to negotiate the price at which they work [...] is to remove one of the vital differences between a democracy and a dictatorship'. In his report to the December GEC, printed in the same issue of the TGWU *Record*, Cousins attacked another aspect of government policy: the dangers likely to arise from the government's proposals for membership of the European Economic Community (EEC). The Treaty of Rome's limits on government expenditure and investment would pose 'serious problems of regional investment and indeed for getting enough investment at home'.

Jack Jones resumed the attack in the February 1967 issue of the *Record*. 'Frank Cousin's resignation as Minister of Technology was a symbol of the fact that technology, expansion and social justice have been given second place to a dogmatic limitation of wages [...] to the defence of the pound and the petrification of the grandiose world military role Labour inherited from the Tories'. Jones lambasted 'the reclassification of certain normal trade union activities as criminal' and attacked those in the party who claimed that the government's actions represented 'social planning': 'over-estimating this, they underestimate the great tradition of independent working-class power'.[7]

Cousins and Jones clearly perceived that there was a battle to be fought and won both in the Labour Party and in the union itself. There remained a strong base of support in the union for their policies of peace, internationalism and workers' rights – but it was not unchallenged. At the 1967 biennial conference the motion for disbanding NATO and the Warsaw Pact was carried 'overwhelmingly' – as were motions calling for opposition to the US war in Vietnam and cuts in defence expenditure. But only three branches actually submitted motions in support of disbanding NATO. Although there were 14 opposing the war in Vietnam, a majority came from just three regions: London, Midlands and Scotland (now under Ray McDonald emerging as a Left-supporting region). No motions came from branches in the South East, the South West, Wales or Yorkshire. The report of the debate notes opposition from those who saw the motion as an 'attack on America' and an intervention from Cousins in which he noted that technically 'the United States was not at war with Vietnam and if we support the US generals who want to use atomic bombs, then we are against humanity'.[8]

There were many more motions opposing the Labour government's Prices and Incomes Board. But again the majority was from just three

7 TGWU *Record*, February 1967.

8 MRC MSS 126/TG/1887/22, Minutes and Record of the 22nd Biennial Delegate Conference, July 1967.

regions. London, the Midlands and Scotland submitted 33. Only 27 came from the other ten regions combined and only one each from the South West, Wales and the East.

This biennial conference was held against a background of sharply worsening economic conditions. At the December 1967 GEC Cousins described the preceding period as one of 'extreme difficulty' – with unemployment returning to the 1962 level, inflation rising to 4.5 per cent and the government attempting to enforce limits to pay rises well below that. It had also cut aspects of social expenditure and raised prescription charges. By April 1968 Jack Jones was warning about a disintegration of support for the Labour Party. The TGWU *Record* had printed the three letters from union members disillusioned with the party. In response Jones wrote: 'the concept of Labour as a trade union party is not merely a historical fact; it has to be a vital part of our political and economic policies if we are to demonstrate that the concept of a mass working-class party based on socialist policies can be successful in terms of social justice and prosperity for ordinary people'. He went to attack the government's incomes policy as threatening Labour 'as a party of and for working people'.[9]

Two months later the *Record* printed a statement from Brian Nicholson as member of the Region 1 Docks Group Regional Committee condemning the strike by dockers at the West India Dock in support of Enoch Powell: 'the action of men at the West India and St Katherine's Dock in striking and demonstrating on behalf of Mr Enoch Powell has done enormous damage to the dockers' cause which we will not find easy to live down. It is not those who are at the bottom of the social ladder – the coloured worker – who are responsible for our present problems'.[10] Another account indicates support even in the liaison committee's stronghold of the Royal Docks. Danny Lyons, representing the liaison committee, failed in his attempt to face down those supporting the Anti-Immigration League – resulting in a majority vote for a withdrawal of labour. Because of the majority vote, and the wider democratic principles at stake, some did stay away from work that day though quite a number did not and the liaison committee did not provide pickets. When interviewed in 1990 another member of the liaison committee, Micky Fenn, commented 'It was the only time I felt really ashamed to be a Docker and when I watched it on television I felt really sick, I mean it was disgraceful'.[11]

While the actual number who went on the march was in fact very small, no more than 200 according to the Ministry of Labour *Gazette*, the

9 Jack Jones, 'Trade unions and the Labour Party', TGWU *Record*, April 1968.

10 TGWU *Record*, June 1968 (Nicholson was later revealed as an MI5 informer: 'Dockers' Leader Passed Strike Tactics to MI5 Agents During National Stoppage', *The Guardian*, 1 January 2001.

11 'Dockers against Racism: An Interview With Micky Fenn', *Race and Class*, 2016, vol.58, no.1, pp.55–60.

publicity provided by the right-wing and pro-Conservative press did indeed do 'enormous damage'. The numbers marching to protest at the House of Commons were, it appears, augmented by members of the National Front – and this also appears to be the case with the parallel march led by some porters from Smithfield. Nonetheless, the fact that traditionally militant workforces, organised by the TGWU, were represented as taking stridently racist positions underlined the fears expressed earlier by Jones and Cousins that the failure of the Labour Party to champion the interests of working people – indeed to all appearances attacking them – was, in deteriorating economic conditions, allowing divisive and anti-working-class sentiments to emerge. Indeed, it was the Labour government itself that provided the context for Powell's 'rivers of blood' speech. The previous month, in March 1968, it had introduced an explicitly racist immigration act, the Commonwealth Immigrants Act, which limited immigration to those with at least one grandparent born in Britain. It was an Act opposed by a sizeable group of left-wing MPs.

The TGWU and Black Workers

Graham Stevenson

The TGWU's 1967 biennial conference made a special feature of its debate on race discrimination led by Matt Folarin.[12] It was no doubt organised with memories of the 1965 biennial where considerable pre-conference discussion was required to dissuade the London Bus Group from tabling a motion opposing any further employment of 'immigrants'. It also followed a period when there had been a spate of disputes in which, in some areas at least, the TGWU had failed to take a stand against racist attitudes and demands.

The 1950s had seen the Conservative government supporting immigration from Commonwealth countries. The TUC issued its first declaration of opposition to 'colour prejudice wherever it may occur' in 1955 and repeated it thereafter. As a policy it gained, at least initially, only limited traction in the trade union movement. Significant discrimination continued in employment and access to housing.[13] Many of the new citizens sought employment in transport and other occupations organised by the TGWU where limited initial occupational qualifications were required. In at least some towns quotas appear to have been imposed within bus transport by informal agreement between managers and the

---

12 TGWU *Record*, September 1967.
13 Stephen Fielding, 'Brotherhood and the Brothers: Responses to "Coloured" Immigration in the British Labour Party *c.* 1951–1965', *Journal of Political Ideologies*, 1998, vol.3, no.1, pp.79–97.

union either at officer or workplace level. In Wolverhampton buses in 1955 there was a 5 per cent limit – later increased. In Coventry in 1958 there was a similar limit.[14] In Bristol non-white workers were totally excluded – a practice challenged in a long-running campaign by Caribbean and Indian workers between 1961 and 1965. This campaign was given support by some in the trade union movement and more generally by the Left in the Labour Party including the local MP, Tony Benn, before the ban was lifted by the city council (see separate panel). Local TGWU officers had in general supported the ban in response to what they claimed was the will of their members.[15]

In Wolverhampton the refusal of the council's transport managers to permit the wearing of turbans triggered a long-running dispute with the Sikh community, running from 1965 to 1968. This dispute formed part of the background to Powell's 1968 speech – a speech which Powell made as local MP in Wolverhampton with careful preparation to maximise local and national impact.[16] In this case the local TGWU officer gave support to the council transport committee in banning turbans while a poll of the TGWU members themselves revealed a majority, though a small one, against the ban. In Wolverhampton, and in the campaign against a similar ban in Manchester, a crucial part of the campaign was the mobilisation of the Sikh community internationally including threats of industrial action against multinational firms in India itself. In Wolverhampton the right to wear a turban was conceded later in 1968 (partly as a result of the shift of control to a regional transport authority) and in Manchester in 1969. Elsewhere, as in Glasgow, the wearing of turbans does not appear to have become an issue.[17]

The mid-1960s also witnessed battles by black workers – especially those from the Indian subcontinent – to secure trade union rights in unorganised or poorly organised workplaces. These battles revealed varying degrees of trade union backing. Some were well supported by the TGWU – as that in a Wolverhampton factory in 1964 led by West Indian and Sikh workers and subsequently described by TGWU officer Brian Mathers, later regional secretary. This particular dispute resulted in a frontal attack on racist practices in the company.[18] Elsewhere in the West Midlands, particularly in the iron foundries, collective organisation was spearheaded by the Indian Workers Association under the leadership of

14 Fielding, 'Brotherhood and the Brothers'.

15 Madge Dresser, *Black and White on the Buses* (Bristol Broadsides, 1986).

16 George Kassimeris, 'Negotiating Race and Religion in the West Midlands: Narratives of Exclusion and Inclusion', *Contemporary British History*, 2017, vol.31, no.3, pp.343–365.

17 Roger Seifert and Andrew Hambler, 'Wearing the Turban: The 1967–1969 Sikh Bus Drivers' Dispute in Wolverhampton', *HSIR*, 2016, vol.37, no.1, pp.83–111.

18 Robert Leeson, *Strike: A Live History* (Allen and Unwin, 1973), p.216.

Jagmohan Joshi and initially either independently of the TGWU or other unions or with little or no support. At the Coneygre Foundry in Tipton in autumn 1968 the company sought to enforce redundancies on Indian members, already members of the TGWU, rather than the white workers in the Amalgamated Foundry Workers Union. This was in defiance of the accepted last-in, first-out principle and the call from the Indian workers that the fall in demand be met by job sharing and a reduced working week. The Indian workers struck work with wider support mobilised by the Indian Workers Association and only minimal assistance from the TGWU. After two months' strike action, and picketing to resist the importation of scabs by the firm, the principle of job sharing was won.[19] This pattern appears to have been relatively typical of the foundry industry in the West Midlands, with the initiative taken by the Indian Workers Association.[20]

A similar failure to provide union support occurred at the Woolf rubber factory in Southall (Region 1) where a largely Sikh workforce had been recruited from India in the 1950s. These workers proved particularly militant and had by 1964 compelled the firm to accept union recognition. In October 1965 the workers went on strike to protest against a dismissal and the failure of the firm to honour a previous agreement to continue pay pending investigation. This led, with the backing of the Indian Workers Association, to a dispute that continued into the early months of 1966 with over 600 workers on strike. The No 1 regional secretary failed to declare the strike official, using the pretext that some strikers were not yet in compliance with the two-year union membership rule, and also decided against the alternative practice of agreeing grants equivalent to strike pay. The failure to declare the strike official also made it more difficult to halt deliveries to the firm. In the end it was the scale of picketing by other local Indian workers that eventually brought the strike to a successful conclusion. But the anger remained. Summer 1966 saw an enquiry under Harry Nicholas, still acting general secretary, that hid the actions of regional officials under a cloak of 'language difficulties'. It also highlighted the difference in practice between Region 1 – where Deakin era full-timers were still dominant – and Region 5 (Midlands) where grants equivalent to dispute benefit had been made to the largely Asian workforce of Stirling Metals of Nuneaton over the same period by assistant general secretary Jack Jones.[21]

---

19 John Wrench, 'Unequal Comrades', Policy Papers in Ethnic Relations, No.5, April 1986, Centre for Research in Ethnic Relations, University of Warwick.

20 Mark Duffield, 'Rationalization and the Politics of Segregation: Indian Workers in Britain's Foundry Industry, 1945–62', *Immigrants and Minorities*, 1985, vol.4, no.2, pp.142–172.

21 MRC MSS 126/TG/1186/A/44, GEC minutes, minute 326, 14 April 1966, and GEC minutes 10 June 1966, Appendix III.

In the East Midlands old discriminatory attitudes remained dominant at workplace and officer level into the early 1970s and were brutally exposed during the Imperial Typewriter dispute in 1974. The mainly female Asian workers went on strike after discovering discrimination in bonus payments as well as recruitment. Neither the elected shop stewards committee, the TGWU convener nor the local TGWU officer gave support. A nine-week strike by the Asian workers, largely sustained by the Indian Workers Association and other Asian organisations, eventually secured victory and the bonus system was rectified by the company. An internal (and unpublished) enquiry by the TGWU made clear the union's condemnation. At least one early retirement at officer level followed.[22]

The TGWU's local failure to support Asian workers at Imperial Typewriters represented the last major episode in which the union capitulated to racist attitudes. As we have seen, the Left leadership of the union, represented by Cousins and then Jones, had, much earlier, made clear their anti-racist commitment and had sought to combat racist views. Cousins himself, on retirement in 1969, became chair of the Race Relations Board. It is also clear that by the early 1970s something of a turning point had been reached across the union – marked by the active involvement of local branches and trades and labour councils in campaigns against the National Front. In 1975, as will be seen in Volume 5, TGWU branches and regions gave massive support to the mainly Asian women workers at Grunwick. London dockers from the 'Royals' marched to the picket line in solidarity.

The reasons for this transformation will become apparent in later chapters and should remind us that class solidarity is not something that is automatic or ever present.[23] On the contrary, it needed to be constantly re-won in new conditions. Equally we should be reminded by the interventions of Enoch Powell, supported by significant sections of the press and the Tory Party right wing, that those who oppose the interests of the working class will also use every instrument they can to sow division. This was particularly so in the late 1960s when it was the TGWU that was leading the main challenge to right-wing policies.

22 Pippa Virdee, 'From the Belgrave Road to the Golden Mile: The Transformation of Asians in Leicester', *From Diasporas to Multi-Locality: Writing British Asian Cities*, Working Paper WBAC 006, 2009 (cited with the kind permission of the author).

23 Satnam Virdee, 'A Marxist Critique of Black Radical Theories of Trade Union Racism', *Sociology*, 2000, vol.34, no.3, pp.545–565.

The Bristol Bus Boycott 1963

On 29 April 1963 Bristol's West Indian Development Committee announced a boycott of Bristol's buses run by the state-owned Bristol Omnibus Company. The Committee did so in response to the company's refusal to employ any drivers or conductors from the city's black community. Three months later, on 27 August, the boycott ended with the company reversing its policy and announcing it would henceforth recruit from all the city's ethnic minorities. The following week two West Indians, one Sikh and two drivers from Pakistan were recruited (Dresser, *Black and White* on the Buses (Bristol Broadsides, 1986))..

The boycott is important for three reasons. First, it was organised by the city's West Indian community itself and was done in a highly strategic manner, drawing on the experience of the 1955 Montgomery bus boycott in the United States and doing so at the height of the US campaign for civil rights. Martin Luther King's 'I have a dream' speech was delivered the day after the victory in Bristol. Second, this victory was secured by mobilising wider support from within the city's population as a whole, particularly from within the Labour Party and with support from one of the city's MPs, Tony Benn, and subsequently from the party's leader Harold Wilson. It also won active intervention by the High Commissioner from Trinidad and Tobago, the ex-Test cricketer Learie Constantine. And it led fairly directly to two Acts of Parliament by the incoming Labour government, the Race Relations Act of 1965 and the second Race Relations Act of 1968. Third, the campaign itself was opposed by the TGWU at South West regional level and this opposition was largely the result of the position taken by the 600 TGWU members employed on the city's buses to exclude black workers. It represented the most high-profile example of racist practice within the union, either tacit or explicit.

As documented elsewhere, racist exclusions and, more commonly, the imposition of employment quotas, though not unchallenged, were relatively widespread in the early 1960s. In some cities, such as Liverpool and Glasgow, TGWU members had, on the contrary, played an important part in opposing such practices. In Bristol, however, with a core of low-paid employment in the docks and transport, this does not seem to have been the case. The previous year, in 1962, physical conflict had erupted among the stevedores in the Bristol docks, resulting in the exclusion of black workers (Madge Dresser, *The Avonmouth Dispute 1962*, www.EnglandsPastforEveryone.org.uk/Explore).

The South West regional secretary, Ron Nethercott, was caught in the middle of the bus dispute. At British level the union opposed racial discrimination in line with TUC policy (as decided in 1955) and had sought to resist motions to biennial conferences opposing immigration. Yet TGWU members locally argued that opening recruitment would further depress their already low wages. The regional secretary unsuccessfully sought to lower the temperature by arguing for behind the scenes negotiations and unwisely criticised the high-profile campaign led by Paul Stephenson on behalf of the West Indian Development Association, leading to a libel action which he lost.

The boycott victory, and the publicity it brought, did, however, mark a turning point in both attitudes and very soon in legislation. While the impetus came from outside the union, it undoubtedly accelerated a change in attitudes within it – and resulted in a more active determination to resist the political use of racism by elements within the Conservative Party later in the decade.

Graham Stevenson was the TGWU's National Secretary for Transport 1999 to 2008 and Vice President of the European Transport Workers Federation.

The Difficult Fight to Secure a Radical Member-led Union

January 1969 saw the declaration of results for the election of a new general secretary ahead of Frank Cousins's retirement. Jack Jones received 334,000 votes. His nearest competitors, Robert Davies and Tim O'Leary received 28,000 and 27,000 respectively. The new political perspectives of a militant 'member-led' union represented by Cousins and Jones appeared to have taken root.

But Jones was well aware of the battles ahead. His leading article in the January issue of the *Record* focused pointedly on Enoch Powell now advocating the reform of trade union law in very similar tones to the Labour leadership. Jones singled out Powell's speech at Solihull on 1 November 1968. Powell had

> attacked the whole concept of union bargaining and local produc-tivity agreements. Some, he said, were merely devices to get round the Incomes Policy [...] Now what does this 'reform of the law' that Powell calls for mean – who will it affect? [...] the people it will affect will be the dockers, the market porters – any industrial workers who have obtained some protection for themselves.[24]

Jones was calling for a class response, in terms of the defence of basic union freedoms, from those who just a few months before had been marching in the opposite direction. He was doing so at the beginning of a year, 1969, that would indeed demand such a class response from all workers.

This chapter has sought to document some of the complex undercur-rents within the TGWU and more generally within the labour movement

---

24 TGWU *Record*, January 1969.

during the latter half of the 1960s. The task facing Jack Jones was no easy one. Hopes for a radical Labour government had collapsed and any talk of transforming industry on workers' terms had been abandoned. Instead trade unionists were being blamed for inflation, trade union rights compromised and incomes policy used to inflict cuts in real incomes on many workers, particularly those not able to use 'unofficial' bargaining pressure. And this division the government was actively seeking to exploit.

Our examination of commercial road transport underlined the complexity of the union's transformation. Attitudes in the North West moved towards a more combative class orientation and in the Midlands towards a less political trade identity but one that nonetheless prioritised 100 per cent trade union membership. In London priority was given to the defence of sectional trade loyalties whether or not they involved conflict with other union members. Even among the London dockers there was considerable variation – between the Royal Docks, stronghold of the liaison committee, and the West India Docks which O'Leary considered his own base and which, as we saw, gave some support to Enoch Powell in 1968.

Moreover, inside the union itself the battle was not won. Often, at best, only lip service was paid to the new direction of a member-led union as pursued by Cousins and Jones. A majority of regions still had secretaries appointed by Deakin and so did a number of the key trade groups: docks, commercial transport, motors. A closer examination of the general secretary election results demonstrates a substantial vote against Jack Jones. Although no individual candidate came anywhere near him, the opposition vote was split between nine contenders whose total support came to just under 200,000.

In this context it should also be remembered that none of this occurred in a political vacuum. Employers' associations closely monitored Left–Right developments within trade unions, advised by bodies such as the Economic League, and gave at least tacit support to right-wing contenders for trade union positions.[25] We can also be sure that the Information Research Department, mainly run by MI5, continued its work – now revealed in terms of its covert use of TV and press over an eight-year period to subvert the Left in the ETU and with clear indications of similar activity against the Left in the National Union of Seamen and, with additional support from within the judiciary, against Jack Dash's unofficial liaison committee among the dockers. Scanlon's election as president of the engineering union in March 1967 was critical in shifting the balance within the TUC and supplying Cousins with a major ally. But Scanlon's election required three ballots. The two previous ballots were

---

25 The Economic League was founded in 1919 to combat left-wing subversion. It was closed down in 1993 following a parliamentary enquiry that exposed its role in the systematic victimisation of trade union militants.

ruled unsafe by the dominant right wing on the executive. Yet although on each occasion the mass circulation press intervened against Scanlon, he still won.[26] The ground was shifting in Britain's big workplaces.

26 J. David Edelstein and Malcolm Warner, *Comparative Union Democracy* (Routledge, 1979).

5

'Democracy [...] Is the Way
to Industrial Peace'[1]

*In which new movements for social change and equality emerge
and the trade union movement forces the Labour government to
abandon its anti-trade union legislation*

Dagenham

The Ford plant at Dagenham was built in 1931. Its purpose was to target
the European and British Empire car markets at a time when the US
market was in deep recession. The plant covered 485 acres of reclaimed
Essex marshland bordering the Thames – with its own power station, steel
plant and docks – and by 1937 it was producing 37,000 cars a year. It was
non-union.

During the war, in line with the requirements set by Bevin as Minister
of Labour, unions were permitted to organise. This continued after the
war. But the character of Ford's industrial relations and the nature of
its production system was quite distinct from the rest of the British car
industry. Ford paid by time not piece. Pay bargaining was excluded from
the shop floor and took place at national level with representatives of the
recognised unions: 22 by the 1950s. Output was maximised by increasing
the speed of the line. Between 1950 and the early 1960s the output of
cars at Dagenham was increased by 180 per cent. Employment went up
by only 18 per cent. By the early 1960s the total workforce was just below
50,000.

In 1953 Ford took over Briggs, a separate firm on the same site
producing car bodies. Briggs paid by the piece in line with the rest of the

---

1 Jack Jones, TGWU *Record*, March 1969.

motor industry, was strongly unionised and had an active shop stewards committee. Ford immediately switched the Briggs pay system into line with that elsewhere at Dagenham, but its shop stewards maintained their function of representing the interests of workers on the line and significantly strengthened the organisation of shop stewards elsewhere in the Ford plant. During the post-Suez recession the Ford management sought to shed staff and used the occasion, and the resulting resistance, to sack the convener of the old Briggs body plant for holding a meeting in a lunch break. A Ministry of Labour court of inquiry found in favour of Ford and condemned communist influence among the shop stewards. It reported that the shop stewards committee operated virtually free of union control – largely because each steward represented workers from a multiplicity of unions and saw themselves, and were seen, as representing the workers in general and not particular unions.[2] Despite the 1957 sackings the shop stewards organisation across the entire plant continued to expand and by 1960 the committee was publishing 50,000 copies weekly of its *Voice of the Ford Worker.*[3]

In 1960 the Ford Company moved to take total control of its British subsidiary and to integrate the Dagenham plant more closely into its global structures. It sought to tighten managerial control and further speed production lines – using as a yardstick the 'Cologne model' set at Ford's German plants employing largely immigrant workers with very limited rights. Strikes at Dagenham escalated. Days lost went up from 100,000 (two days a year per worker) in 1960 to 400,000 in 1962. During the recession of that year Ford again sought redundancies, and again used the resulting turmoil to sack a leading steward, Bill Francis. This, and the threat of redundancies, precipitated an unofficial strike.

The minutes of the TGWU's London and South East Region for 29–30 January 1963 record as follows:

> it became clear the Management intended to insist on a degree of redundancy with a view to getting rid of certain workers who were regarded as uncooperative. This was an untenable position and whilst not wishing to be involved in a stoppage of work if this could be avoided it was nonetheless made quite clear following a meeting of the Finance and General Purposes Committee that support would be given to our members if we became involved in an official withdrawal of labour from 17 November. At the request of the AEU, however, a meeting of executive representatives of

2 Ministry of Labour (G.C. Cameron) Court of Inquiry, 1957, Cmnd, 131, Parlimentary paper.

3 H.A. Turner, G. Clack and G Roberts, *Labour Relations in the Motor Industry* (Routledge, 1967), p.290.

interested unions [...] was held on 14th November resulting in a decision to defer the proposed withdrawal of labour.

A further meeting on 19 November agreed to discuss 'individual cases'.[4]

Kevin Halpin, union convener for the body shop, explains what happened next: 'after discussions the 700 sacked was reduced to 300. There was no negotiated resumption and all the stewards were still on the other side of the gate [...] after further negotiation another 250 workers were taken back. It became evident that each person was being screened'.[5] An official strike was called early in 1963. The Minister of Labour intervened to hold an enquiry. Chaired by the notably anti-union Professor D.T. Jack, it produced a report that was strongly hostile to the shop stewards and upheld the right of the firm to exclude those who it understood to be 'disloyal or disruptive'.[6] It was clear that the still right-wing-led AEU was siding with the management – with Bill Carron, its general secretary, writing in the Ford Company house magazine, attacking communists in the same tones as Arthur Deakin a decade before.

The victimised stewards remained on the street. However, solidarity continued. Members of the TGWU in the London wholesale markets ensured that they did not go hungry. Kevin Halpin again: the 'TGWU regional office told us we should buy meat from Smithfield, fruit and vegetables from Covent Garden and fish from Billingsgate [...]. Many mornings we opened the boxes from Billingsgate [...] and we found salmon, halibut and Dublin Bay prawns all of which were then caught wild and very expensive'. Similarly the meat boxes from Smithfield contained prime cuts of game – all 'marked incorrectly'.[7]

Halpin concludes with an incident from the last day of the court of inquiry when he went into a pub to 'collect his thoughts'. To his surprise he found a group of the new conveners drinking with Leslie Blakeman, the Ford personnel manager. 'What was I to do? Raving would surely give him too much satisfaction. One of the conveners was at the bar and bought me a pint. I returned the round next time and asked the conveners what Blakeman was drinking [...]. He sipped the pint with an ashen face'.[8]

4 MRC MSS 964/2/10, London and South East TGWU region minutes, 29–30 January 1963.

5 Halpin, *Memoirs*, pp.70–71

6 Ministry of Labour (D.T. Jack), Court of Inquiry, 1963, Cmnd.1999, Parliamentary paper.

7 Halpin, Memoirs, p.71.

8 Haplin, *Memoirs*; H. Beynon, *Working for Ford* (Penguin, 1975) in an otherwise important and useful study claims that Kevin Halpin and his fellow stewards on the Left and in the Communist Party failed to mobilise continuing support for industrial action and infers that this was in order to secure electoral preferment to executive positions in the AEU and elsewhere. Beynon appears not to understand the importance

The following year the speed-up at Dagenham was intensified. However, only 3,400 days were lost through strike action: one twelfth of a day per worker through the year. Without its left-wing leadership the shop stewards committee temporarily lost direction – but only temporarily. Halpin himself eventually found employment in ship repair in the London docks and by 1966 had become chair of the LCDTU, an organisation that would play a key part in rallying the trade union movement to defeat anti-trade union legislation in 1969 and again in 1972.

Women's Rights and the Long Fight for Equal Pay

Mary Davis

Despite government inaction, the campaign for equal pay continued after the war. During the period of the post-war Labour government, the TUC did not support the campaign. At its Congress in 1949, the General Council's statement appeared to advocate abandoning the issue altogether. It said: 'In the light of [...] the continuing need for counter-inflationary policies, the committee decided that a further approach by the TUC to the government on equal pay would be inappropriate at the present time'.[9]

It was thus hardly surprising that during the period of the Labour government, however, no improvement was made and the gap between men's and women's earnings was, on average, 50 per cent.

If any progress at all was to be made on equal pay it would be up to individual unions to press for it – a somewhat forlorn hope at least until the 1950s when white-collar unions in the public sector, under pressure from their women members, engaged in an intensive campaign which resulted in 1955 in a government announcement that it would attempt to equalise pay in the public sector.

Thus, until the Ford strike in 1968, the campaign for equal pay was centred almost exclusively on the public sector, and it was among these women workers that some modest gains can be recorded. It was hoped in particular that women teachers and women civil servants would win equal pay, given that the 1946 report of the Royal Commission had expressly recommended this. In fact, women teachers had to wait until 1961 before they achieved equal pay. In the case of women civil servants, after mass public campaigning, including demonstrations and petitions, a scheme was introduced in 1955 to establish equal rates of pay for men and women

---

of the Left's wider strategy of shifting the balance of power within key unions such as the AEU – without which the defeat of the 1970–1974 Conservative government is unlikely to have been achieved: Seifert and Sibley, *Revolutionary Communist*.

9 Bridlington Congress, TUC Congress Report 1969, TUC Library Collections at London Metropolitan University.

doing equal work in the non-industrial civil service. However, this was to be achieved gradually over seven years.

However inadequate the settlement, the principle of conceding equal pay to civil servants inevitably encouraged the aspirations of many other women in public sector employment. In 1956, the Union of Post Office Workers announced to their conference that they had negotiated an agreement with the employers in which women staff had the option of either full equal pay providing they accept 'liability for all duties and attendances associated with the work' (this included night duties),[10] or to retain existing conditions of service and thereby obtain 95 per cent of male rate. The pattern that emerged in this and similar agreements is that women could obtain equal pay for the same work on the same conditions as men. Given that the vast majority of women worked in segregated areas of employment, they were clearly excluded and thus it was unsurprising that from the mid-1950s all three parties in Parliament declared formally, at least, in favour of equal pay. However, apart from some professional women, some local government workers and some women civil servants, the 1950s was a bleak decade for women workers, with nothing done to apply the principle of equal pay to the private sector. Government and trade unions appeared to accept the dubious argument that the British economy would collapse if women obtained pay parity with men.

In the 1960s, parallel but almost unconnected with the industrial battles besetting Labour and Tory governments, the long fight for equal pay for women continued. The Labour Party manifesto for 1964 general election called for a Charter of Rights for all employees to include 'the right to equal pay for equal work'. Having neglected the issue since the first equal pay resolution was passed in 1888, the TUC Congress in September 1965 followed the Labour Party lead with a resolution reaffirming 'its support for the principles of equality of treatment and opportunity for women workers in industry, and calls upon the General Council to request the government to implement the promise of "the right to equal pay for equal work" as set out in the Labour Party election manifesto'.[11]

The Labour Party's election pledge may have been prompted by its desire to join the EEC so that it would be in compliance with the Treaty of Rome's clause requiring member states to adopt the principle of equal pay for women. However, the application was rejected and thus the Wilson government shelved the issue. Equal pay may have been forgotten for another decade or two were it not for the action of women trade unionists, this time in the private sector.

10 Union of Post Office Workers Special Report on Equal Pay (Telephonists & Telegraphists), p.3, Part of the Agenda of National Conference, Margate 1956, The Women's Library, London School of Economics.
11 TUC Congress Report 1965, TUC Library Collections at London Metropolitan University.

Women's Strikes at Ford 1968: Dagenham and Halewood

In 1968 women sewing machinists at Ford's Dagenham and Halewood factories went on strike over a regrading demand. In the course of a general regrading exercise, management informed the women who made the seat covers for Ford cars that their jobs were now to be graded in Category B (less skilled production jobs), instead of Category C (more skilled production jobs), and that they would be paid 15 per cent less than the full B rate received by men. Clearly this was not a case of women doing the same work as the men, although their argument was that it required equal skill. This was well testified by Maureen Jackson, one of the women machinists:

> If our work built up and they didn't need so many car seats, they would say to some of the girls, 'Oh, we'd like you to go over to the door panels, because they're a bit short-staffed', and the girls would go over there and get stuck in and do the door panels, or in the tank shop; they would find you work over there, but when we were very busy and there was quite a few spare machines, they could never say to the men, 'Would you come over and do a bit of machining?', because, you know, the men would never have a clue how to even thread a needle, I shouldn't think, rather than do machining, and in the end the women started talking amongst theirselves and saying, 'Well, this is not on; we can sort of turn our hands to anything but the men can't'.[12]

What started as an overtime ban was followed in May 1968 by an unofficial one-day strike by 187 women at the Dagenham plant, quickly escalating into an all-out stoppage. This was precipitated by Ford management's threatening letter to the women warning them that they had breached their contract. The Dagenham strike was joined ten days later by a walk-out of 180 women in Liverpool at Ford's Halewood plant. The strike lasted three weeks

Bernie Passingham, TGWU and the joint union convenor, who had supported the women's claim and the strike from its inception, acknowledged the slow response of the women's union, the National Union of Vehicle Builders (NUVB).[13] He felt that the women 'got totally ignored' and 'that some of our national officials, they didn't agree with what we were doing, they didn't think it was right. And so we, particularly myself,

---

12 TUC equal pay archive: Recording Women's Voices, TUC History Online: The Union Makes Us Strong.

13 The NUVB merged with the TGWU in 1972.

Figure 3: Women sewing machinists on strike at Fords, Dagenham
(Unite Photo Archive)
Credit: TUC Library Collections

had to push them aside'.[14] He was particularly referring to his own union which was slow to make the strike official.

The strike brought all production at Ford to a standstill. This, of course, was a major blow to Ford's owners who were losing £1.25 million each day of the strike. They expressed their concerns to the government, thus prompting the intervention of Barbara Castle, the Secretary of State for Employment and Productivity in Harold Wilson's government. She brokered a deal which ended the strike three weeks after it began. Although the deal increased their rate of pay to 7 per cent below that of men (it was 15 per cent below prior to the strike), the women still earned only 92 per cent of the male Category B rate, rising to the full Category B rate the following year. Thus they did not win their original demand that they

14   Quoted in Jonathan Moss, 'Women, Workplace Militancy and Political Subjectivity in Britain, 1968–1985', unpublished PhD thesis (Glasgow University, 2015), p.70.

be moved to Category C (more skilled production jobs). A court of inquiry (under the Industrial Courts Act 1919), chaired by Jack Scamp, was also set up to consider the sewing machinists' regrading, but this did not find in women's favour. The women were only regraded into Category C following a further six-week strike in 1984.

Rose Boland, one of the Dagenham machinists' shop stewards, expressed her disillusionment with the outcome of the 1968 strike, saying: 'although we did get more money, we did not gain the point, we won a battle, but lost the war'.[15]

Nonetheless, despite the outcome, the Ford women's strike was both groundbreaking and inspirational. Its most important significance, however, was that it marked the beginning of the campaign for equal pay in the hitherto neglected private sector. The Ford strike led to a number of other equal pay strikes and the formation by women trade unionists and others of the National Joint Action Campaign Committee for Women's Equal Rights (NJACCWER).

A huge groundswell of protest against government and trade union inaction began to manifest itself. In 1968, against General Council advice, an amendment to a motion on equal pay was passed which called for TUC affiliates to support any union taking strike action for equal pay. The TUC even held a one-day conference on equal pay in November 1968. Most unions by this time had declared forcefully in favour of equal pay and appeared to be keen to do something at long last for their women members. As has been previously noted in this volume, TGWU policy was supportive of the demand for equal pay. One of its strongest advocates was Frank Cousins who, according to his biographer, was committed to recruiting more women members in the union.[16] He understood that equal pay could not be achieved unless women were organised and men supported them, a position for which he strongly argued at the 1969 biennial conference.

'This', Cousins told conference, 'was no marginal problem [...] the unequal payment that employers were asserting was the right to make more profit out of women than out of men [...] experience has shown that equal pay could be achieved when women were organised, were ready to press for it and had the support of the men'. Jack Jones replied 'to the delegates who argued that the union should not encourage women to work when they should be looking after their children. Tens of thousands of women had no choice'. In his conference closing speech Cousins gave the example of talking to a woman bus driver in the Soviet Union. 'I said to her that some people argued that in socialism the men would drive the buses and the women would be the conductors. Her reply was "Well, my idea of socialism

---

15 Moss, 'Women, Workplace Militancy', p.91.
16 Goodman, *Awkward Warrior*, p.44.

is where I drive the bus and he is the conductor" [...] we accept and tolerate the idea that there is such a thing as women's work'.[17]

May 1969 saw a massive equal pay demonstration organised by NJACCWER. Barbara Castle, the employment secretary, in order to forestall further unrest, decided to introduce the Equal Pay Act of 1970. This permitted equal pay claims to be made from women in the public and private sectors if they were engaged in the same or broadly similar work. However, although the act was passed in May 1970, it was not implemented until January 1976, thus allowing employers just over five years in which to make 'adjustments'. Basically this meant that they had nearly six years to regrade jobs in discriminatory ways thus rendering them immune from the very limited scope of the act.

Clearly, the fight for equal pay was far from over and reliance on the law alone, inadequate as it was, was unlikely to achieve results. As many women trade unionists were to show, equal pay could only be fought for, and sometimes won, through the mechanism of collective bargaining and strong union organisation. The Ford strikes and later the successful Trico dispute were two successful examples of the potential power of trade unions when they at last they began to recognise the importance of fighting for all their members – women and men.[18]

Mary Davis is a Visiting Professor of Labour History,
Royal Holloway, University of London
and Secretary for the Marx Memorial Library.

Facing Down a Right-wing Labour Government: Winning the Battle Against Anti-Trade Union Legislation

Economically the years 1968 to 1970 were challenging. Inflation escalated – from 4.6 per cent in 1968 to 5.3 per cent in 1969 to 6.4 per cent in 1970. Unemployment also increased. By 1970 it exceeded 4 per cent, double the 2 per cent at the beginning of the decade. And social services were cut. Roy Jenkins as Chancellor of the Exchequer imposed cash limits on government spending at a time of high inflation. He did so in compliance with conditions set by the IMF for a further crisis loan in 1968, restricting programmes for housing, health and local government services – the first bitter taste of neo-liberal monetarism.

This made the struggle on wages all the more important – but also more difficult, particularly for those in vulnerable and poorly unionised

17 TGWU *Record*, August 1969.
18 G. Stevenson, 'The Forgotten Dispute: equality, discrimination and class in the Trico equal pay dispute', *Labour History Review*, 81 (2).

employment. This was equally so for those in direct or indirect government employment where the government could more easily impose the full force of wage restraint. It also made it important for the TGWU to develop wider alliances, both in the trade union movement and in the Labour Party, to advance alternative perspectives.

The big battle of 1968 was against interventions by the government and the Prices and Incomes Board (PIB) to impose delays of up to a year on agreed wage awards. It did so for bus workers on 'provincial' services outside London, a particularly poorly paid group of workers, who, instead of a pay increase, suffered a 4 per cent cut in real pay across the year. Some took unofficial action. Cousins, mindful of their organisational weakness and the memory of the 1958 London bus strike – a strike defeated by the combined efforts of the government and the TUC right wing – counselled caution and eventually secured a backdated award at the end of the year.[19]

Nonetheless, this episode confirmed his determination to defeat the government's use of the PIB to cut wages. It also firmed up his opposition to those in the TUC leadership, including its general secretary George Woodcock, who supported 'voluntary' wage restraint in line with PIB recommendations. At the Special TUC conference in February 1968 Cousins lined up the TGWU with Scanlon's engineers and came within 500,000 votes of beating the platform – enough to destroy the credibility of Woodcock's support for wage restraint as advocated in the TUC's 'economic review'. Three months later, in June 1968, the names of Frank Cousins and Hugh Scanlon headed the list of signatories of the *Tribune*'s Socialist Charter – a reassertion of the socialist objectives of the Labour Party. This was the first major restatement of the socialist aims of the Labour Party since Cousins's defeat of Gaitskell on Clause 4 and nuclear weapons in 1960. It called for a free trade union movement, socialist planning, public ownership, disarmament, opposition to racial, religious and sex discrimination and 'economic independence' (as against the pending application for EEC membership).[20]

In autumn 1968 Cousins and Scanlon took the battle against pay restraint into the conferences of the TUC and then the Labour Party. In each they won by a landslide. Moving the motion at the Labour Party conference, Cousins argued for opposition to 'any legislation that would curtail basic trade union rights'.[21] The motion was won by 5,098,000 to 1,240,000. The votes reflected rank-and-file anger at government intervention through the year, holding wages to a 3.5 per cent increase at a time when inflation was 4.6 per cent. During these months unofficial action

19 MRC MSS 126 /TG/197/2/1, Passenger Services Group minutes, 20 May 1968.
20 Goodman, *Awkward Warrior*, pp.550–551.
21 Goodman, *Awkward Warrior*, pp.567–68.

– often to ensure that gains in productivity did not go solely to shareholders – complemented official action such as that by the Confederation of Shipbuilding and Engineering Unions. A reinvigorated shop stewards movement was now taking up the banner of social justice dropped by the Labour government.

However, Wilson pressed ahead with plans for further and more punitive legislation. The government had been disappointed by the Royal Commission on Trade Unions chaired by Lord Donovan which reported in summer 1968. Donovan had proposed a more nuanced approach. Instead of legal prohibitions on unofficial strikes, his report argued for drawing shop stewards more directly into the structures of official bargaining, providing recognition and training and thereby, it was hoped, restricting freedom of action. It reflected opinion among industrial relations professionals that formal legal penalties would simply provoke conflict and that more subtle tactics were required.[22]

But it did not satisfy Wilson. He and the right-wingers in the Cabinet wanted legal penalties immediately – and did so, at least partly, under pressure from the IMF, the United States and international finance. A White Paper was drafted in December 1968. It included provisions for a 28-day 'cooling off' period before any strike could take place, powers by the government to enforce ballots and penalties on unofficial strikers. Discussions took place with the new Minister of Labour, Barbara Castle, on 30 December where union leaders united against any attack on shop stewards. Despite this rejection, the White Paper was published virtually unchanged on 15 January.[23] Cousins expressed his anger in an article in the *Sunday Mirror*. 'There has been a growing belief in the ranks of even reasonably minded, middle of the road trade unionists that the Labour government has lost touch with them [...]. [It] is displaying an absolute political aversion and dislike of trade unionists'. Cousins repeated the verdict of the TUC on the White Paper as 'completely misguided and quite unacceptable'.[24] The government had set itself on a 'course of self-destruction'. Writing in the TGWU *Record* a little later, Jack Jones argued that 'Britain's trade unions are too weak – not too strong': 'Democracy, not punitive intervention by ministers and Courts, urged on by the press, is the way to industrial peace'.[25]

The government took no notice. The Chancellor of the Exchequer Roy Jenkins announced in his budget speech on 15 April that the government

22 R. Seifert, 'Big Bangs and Cold Wars: The British Industrial Relations Tradition After Donovan (1965-2015)', *Employee Relations*, 2015, vol.37, no.6, pp.746–760.

23 TNA CAB 129/139/31 and 129/142/2 give the origins of the legislation and detail the governments inflexibility in face of opposition. 129/140/3 and 129/140/7 outline Cabinet opposition from Judith Hart and Richard Crossman.

24 *Sunday Mirror*, 19 January 1969, as quoted in Goodman, *Awkward Warrior*, p.576.

25 TGWU *Record*, March 1969.

intended to legislate immediately with a Short Bill that contained all the most damaging restrictions on trade union freedom. In doing so Jenkins triggered an amazing demonstration of anger across the trade union movement. The first General Strike since 1926 took place on 1 May 1969. It was called by the LCDTU and supported by shop stewards committees and some union district committees from across Britain. It was by no means total. But it was estimated that up to a million workers took part. It covered the core of Britain's industrial working class: the shipyards, engineering works, coalfields and mass production factories from the Clyde and Mersey to the Midlands and London, and followed an earlier protest strike on 27 February.[26]

A special conference of trade union executives, organised by the TUC, followed in June. Lobbied by thousands of shop stewards mobilised by the LCDTU, the conference voiced its implacable opposition to the proposed legislation. On 18 June 1969 the government capitulated. With Cousins due to retire ten weeks later, on 8 September, it was a fitting conclusion to his 15 years as general secretary – a victory won by workers themselves in defence of workers' freedoms.

Jack Jones Takes Over, Making the TGWU 'the Most Democratic Union in the World'[27]

The January 1970 TGWU *Record* appeared for the first time as a tabloid newspaper. This had been a particular project of Jack Jones. He wanted to transform the union's journal into a mass circulation publication with a direct impact in factories and workplaces. Designed by the acclaimed graphic artist Ken Sprague, its pages sparkle with cartoons and graphics emphasising the class nature of British society and the importance of collective organisation to resist. In its first issue Jones set out his manifesto:

> A Tory spokesperson was attacking me the other day. Mr Jones, he said, was not 'controlling his members' at Tilbury and in the British Road Services. Let's get one point straight. The London dockers, the BRS drivers or any other workers are not *my* members or puppets to be controlled from Transport House. They are members of the union, entitled to be involved in taking decisions about agreements that concern themselves [...] The situation at the London docks could have resulted in a major strike; one reason why it hasn't is because all the members, and their representatives,

26 Seifert and Sibley, *Revolutionary Communist*, pp.178–182.
27 This section draws on material very kindly supplied by John Fisher, former TGWU Director of Research and Education.

have been involved in working out the final agreement. A ballot of workers was held. It resulted in the rejection of the offer. What is the complaint? This is why the Union is insisting on shop stewards participation in negotiations. The BRS dispute is another [...] example [...]. It is part of the process of making the TGWU the most democratic union in the world.[28]

Strengthening member democracy had been a key concern of Jack Jones ever since his appointment as acting assistant general secretary in 1964.

His first initiatives were directed against the unwarranted exercise of power by full-time officers, particularly when this excluded shop stewards or involved unduly close relations with managements. During the dock strikes of 1966 Jones first intervened in Hull. There the union was in danger of losing its membership base members as a result of full-time officers being seen as too close to management. Three full-timers were dismissed – an act unprecedented in the union's history. 'Every officer', Jones stressed, 'should be responsible to an elected committee'.[29] Jones followed this by an intervention in the Liverpool docks that asserted the rights of workers' representatives against instructions by full-timers. His most high-profile intervention came later. It was against Les Kealey during the 1969 Ford strike. As trade group secretary for engineering, Kealey was responsible for the motor industry and the most powerful trade group officer in the union. Early in 1969 Ford had sought to impose many of the provisions restricting shop steward freedom contained in the government's White Paper, sparking what was initially an unofficial strike against these 'penal clauses'. Kealey had signed the agreement and in doing so ignored the decisions of two delegate conferences. Jones intervened to repudiate the agreement and Kealey was reprimanded by the General Executive. He resigned soon after. It was a warning to be heeded by all other trade group secretaries from the Deakin period. Kealey's replacement by Moss Evans as trade group secretary ushered in a new era. From then on elected conveners joined any negotiations with the Ford managers, and the venue was shifted from Café Royal to a windowless room in the Ford headquarters.[30]

Jones's second initiative was on the union's internal democracy and was launched from the 1968 Rules Revision conference in which Jones took the leading role. The conference reduced the autonomy of trade group secretaries and, correspondingly, increased the authority of regional committees and, particularly, district committees. It marked a shift from

28 TGWU *Record*, January 1970.
29 Jack Jones, *Union Man: An Autobiography* (Warren and Pell, 2008), p. 181.
30 Jones, *Union Man*, pp.208–209, supplemented by oral testimony from Eddie Roberts, one of the five Ford conveners and representing Halewood.

the pattern of bargaining established by Bevin by which deals were struck at national level with major firms and employers federations. Jones wanted to ensure that the union's structure matched the new bargaining realities, with decisions increasingly taken at local company and plant level and reflecting agreements reached mainly by stewards. The development of district committees in particular enabled much more direct participation by stewards in the work of the union. Additionally, the conference merged Merseyside and the Manchester area regions into a new Region 6 to take effect from January 1970, bringing a new level of radicalism to the combined committee.[31] Finally the Rules Revision conference lifted the Deakin era ban on communists holding offices in the union.[32]

It would be wrong to credit all these moves to Jones as they had the full support and endorsement of Frank Cousins. Organisationally they marked the consolidation of the new type of union that Cousins had brought into being. Jones, however, ensured they were embedded in union rules.

Jones's third area of intervention was in education, ensuring that it matched the union's new structures and that shop stewards were fully equipped with knowledge about the union and industrial relations practices to take on their new roles. Education, which had previously been largely contracted out, was redirected primarily to shop stewards and as far possible locally and on site. When he was Midlands regional secretary, Jones first suggested day-release courses in 1958 specifically for shop stewards in the BMC. The courses which began in Birmingham and Coventry that year were a direct result of his proposal.[33] This was carried forward the following year at national level. In 1959, with Cousins's support, the union introduced a new policy of making sure that TGWU education directly assisted the union's workplace representatives and that it should be firmly rooted in the day-to-day activities of the union's growing number of shop stewards. The growth of in-plant bargaining and 100 per cent membership agreements continued throughout the Jones era, and this in turn led to an increase in the demand for workplace-based and day-release courses.

Earlier Cousins had used his position in the Conservative government's NEDC, and from 1964 as Minister for Technology, to push for government and industry-level support for comprehensive and properly financed training with a direct input from the TUC. The result was the Industrial Training Act of 1964, which included the establishment of a

31 MSS 126/TG/102/1/1, Region No. 6 minutes 1970. The second meeting of the new regional committee on 5 May 1970 elected a delegate to the British Campaign for Peace in Vietnam, passed (though with opposition) a motion condemning the US invasion of Cambodia and also passed a motion to place advertisements in future with the *Morning Star*.

32 Goodman, *Awkward Warrior*, pp.561–565; Jones, *Union Man*, p.199.

33 TGWU *Record*, January 1968, pp.30–35.

National Industrial Training Council with Frank Cousins as one of its members. This Act introduced the practice of day-release for apprentices and trainees. This principle was easily extended to shop stewards. This in turn led to a mushrooming of 'in-plant' and joint courses with employers, and the establishment of the TUC shop stewards' training courses from 1964 onwards – also generally based on day-release – increased the volume of trade union education still further.

The years from 1965 onwards saw an explosion in the number of locally based 'in-plant' courses and day-release courses for shop stewards. In 1968 Frank Cousins sent out a circular encouraging regions to extend one-day training schools for their shop stewards as widely as possible. The union preferred these to be held during working hours where arrangements could be arrived at with employers. There were courses in almost all the major oil, chemical and food-processing companies such as Fry's, Birds Eye, ICI, Shell, Austin's, Midland Red, Lucas, the docks, Waterford Glass and Courtaulds. Courses were organised at Shell Petrochemicals, ICI and British Nylon Spinners in Gloucester and at Wilton on Teesside and at the ICI paint factory at Stowmarket, Manchester and in Scotland.

The result was a far more confident and assertive population of shop stewards, often of a new and younger generation, able to carry forward the union's work in a far more difficult and turbulent period. By the time of the 1974 Cirencester summer school, 65 per cent of the 479 students were *under* 30.[34]

Conclusion: A Labour Government That Had Lost Its Way

In the June 1970 general election the Conservative Party defeated Labour and formed a government with a majority of 30.

The previous four years had witnessed the Wilson government moving into ever sharper conflict with the movement that it was meant to represent. At the union's 1969 biennial conference Cousins had to fend off a resolution calling for the union to end financial support for the Labour Party. 'It would be a severe blow to the Union to disassociate itself from the Labour Party. Labour is not the party of a few politicians. It belongs to all of us [...] to disassociate ourselves from the Labour Party is to break the links with our political philosophy'.[35] Three months later at the Labour Party conference the newly appointed assistant general secretary, Harry Urwin, appealed for a change of direction by the party leadership and a new unity with the unions, in the face of a speech by Barbara Castle announcing

---

34 For more discussion see John Field, 'Learning for Work', in R. Fieldhouse (ed.), *A History of Modern British Adult Education* (NIACE, 1996), pp.333–353.
35 TGWU *Record*, August 1969.

an intention to reactivate parts of the Prices and Incomes Act to control wages. 'Together Labour and the unions could build a partnership giving working men and women a greater say in determining their own wages, preventing irresponsible mass sackings or indirect dismissals'.[36]

The vision of 1964 had been for some form of 'socialist planning' transforming the economy. Wilson's secret deals with the US in 1965 and 1966 had trapped the government into maintaining an unsustainable valuation of the pound and levels of overseas military expenditure that crippled domestic investment. Inevitably, too, big business used the overvalued pound to buy up assets overseas rather than investing at home – and met no opposition from the government. Devaluation when it came was too late to shift this pattern. Spending on housing, health and local government services was curtailed. Inflation increased. The press – as well as the nation's industrial relations industry and the government itself – placed the blame squarely on the unions.

One deeply worrying response to the pressure on wages and social services was the rise in racism. Price inflation impacted worst on workers in a weak bargaining position and where unemployment was once more beginning to emerge. How far there was actually an increase in racism is difficult to assess. As we have noted it was endemic in the 1950s in housing and some areas of employment. What did change, however, was the willingness of politicians on the right wing of the Conservative Party, and not just Enoch Powell, to use it demagogically to seek to build a new populist base within the working class. Despite some serious compromises at local level, the TGWU nationally was solid in its opposition and waged a relatively consistent campaign that stressed the necessity, for the class unity of labour, of opposing racism in any form.

Another consequence of rapidly rising inflation was the mobilisation of women workers. Women often tended to be employed in areas where local productivity bargaining did not operate and where basic national rates left them increasingly disadvantaged. Women were additionally – and far more fundamentally, as Frank Cousins put it at the 1969 biennial – subjected to assumptions about pay that enabled employers to exercise the right to extract more profit from female than male workers. The old type of national agreements reached with big firms and employers' associations inherited from the days of Bevin and Deakin simply copper-fastened these assumptions. Local plant-level bargaining did not necessarily end them. It did, however, provide the context in which women could organise with a new effectiveness. By the end of the 1960s the union was, at last, beginning to give the issue of equality the importance it deserved.

Yet overall these years did see something of a transformation. The emphasis by Cousins and Jones on a member-led union, on union

36 TGWU *Record*, October 1969.

democracy supplanting rule by full-time officers, created a new assertiveness by members. It did so above all, through the tens of thousands of shop stewards that now, with increasing authority, represented the union. They did so jointly, as we have seen, with shop stewards from other unions that had also in the course of the 1960s turned towards the Left, particularly the engineers and the draughtsmen and scientific workers. By 1969–1970, the combined forces of the trade union Left were, as represented in the TUC and the Labour Party, beginning to pose an alternative leadership to that of the right-wing dominated parliamentary party, carrying forward and deepening the challenge thrown down by Frank Cousins in 1960. The workplace fortresses of the working class had, through discussion, debate and direct experience, begun to assemble the forces that would soon defeat a far more determined government.

Some Issues for Discussion

1. How far in these years did the TGWU finally become a 'member-led union', and in what ways might this have been important for its ability to mobilise against 'In Place of Strife' (Cmnd 3888)?

2. How far had the TGWU developed an adequate response to occupational racism by the end of the 1960s? Why had TGWU leaderships failed to intervene effectively before, as, for instance, in the Bristol bus colour bar?

3. Why did income discrimination against women become such a central issue in the late 1960s?

4. How far did the development of 'cross-union' organisations such as the LCDTU change popular assumptions about the nature of the 'working class' in this period?

III

1970–1974

In which TGWU members mobilise a mass movement to defeat a Conservative government

Case studies detail working-class mobilisation on Merseyside, the difficult battle to sustain class unity in Belfast and the revival of working-class militancy in West Lothian

Introduction

The years 1970–1974 saw the high tide of trade union power. For the first time since 1926 the TUC called a General Strike to halt a government attack on workers' rights – and won it.

In this the TGWU played a central role. Jack Jones created the necessary alliances within the trade union movement and made the calls for action. However, he did not do so alone. In all he did he was dependent on the wider changes in the union described in previous chapters: the emergence of a new generation of workplace leaders themselves empowered by fellow workers now demanding wider forms of social justice.

This section will seek to provide an understanding of the profundity of the challenges posed by trade unionists during these years: the inter-union solidarity which won two successive miners' strikes; the wave of workplace occupations that mobilised wider communities around the principle of the right to work; and, most of all, the two-year struggle to assert workers' freedoms and defeat the Industrial Relations Act. Here TGWU members, particularly in the docks, played a central role.

However, this challenge did not occur spontaneously or in a political vacuum. Internationally these four years saw the whole post-war political order fracturing. Working people from Chile to the Middle East, Africa and South East Asia showed themselves no longer content to produce oil, copper, rubber and tin on terms that left them impoverished and starving. The dollar's international grip was challenged and its highly exploitative link to gold abandoned. Western currencies, including the pound, rapidly lost value.

It was these international traumas that in part precipitated major conflicts within the governing class in Britain – splits which significantly assisted the ability of working people to seize the initiative and to project a new political agenda of their own. By 1973 the trade union movement, in large measure through Jack Jones and the TGWU, had been able to win the Labour Party to adopt a programme calling for an 'irreversible shift of wealth and power in favour of working people'.[1] By 1974–1975 this had resulted in legislative action by the incoming Labour government to nationalise motors, aerospace, steel, shipbuilding and to a lesser extent oil, to abolish anti-trade union laws and enact health and safety legislation that for the first time gave trade union representatives direct legal power in the workplace.

Yet here the advance halted. Within five years the tables had been turned. Why was this? How far can we find the origins of this reversal in the period of this volume – in those discussions that took place in 1973 between the TUC and the Labour Party, effectively led by Jack Jones, about the future programme of a Labour government. A new 'social contract' was agreed. It contained many positive commitments. But it was a contract that also implicitly accepted that wages were a cause of inflation and that a key part of future economic management would have to involve legislative controls over wages, something which the TGWU battled against throughout the 1960s.

This section will therefore celebrate some unprecedented victories. At the same time it will also seek to address some of the wider issues of strategy that the working-class movement encountered at the time and still has to resolve today.

1 *Programme for Britain* (Labour Party, 1973).

6

Assembling the Forces for Victory

Liverpool Dockers and Class Solidarity

Within a month of taking office the new Conservative government were faced with a national dock strike, the first official national dock strike in half a century. At a time of very high inflation, the TGWU national docks committee had narrowly rejected an interim wage settlement crafted by Jack Jones and the port employers and had demanded a £20 a week guaranteed wage – prior to Devlin's Stage 2 settlement due later that summer. According to *The Times*, the 39–51 vote was tipped by the 'traditionally militant' Merseyside dockers.[1]

Within a week the government had declared a state of emergency. Within two weeks a court of inquiry had been established. Within three the dockers had emerged with a victory.

In the midst of this crisis, on 1 July 1970, the Employment Minister Robert Carr presented the Cabinet with a review paper on industrial relations. The paper noted that, while disputes in mining had declined over the past decade, disputes elsewhere had increased sharply and in 1969 and 1970 there had been a 'marked acceleration'. Many of these strikes were unofficial and the sections worst affected were 'docks, motor assembly and components and shipbuilding'. There was also a worrying tendency for a resort to strike action among non-manual workers. Doctors, teachers and other white-collar occupations 'have threatened or taken strike action for the first time'. This 'high level of militancy' had been reflected in the high settlements of between 10 and 11 per cent over the past six months.[2]

The paper then went to note the changing character of trade union leaderships and structures. 'The present leaders of the two largest unions,

1 *The Times*, 1 July 1970.
2 TNA CAB 129/150/7, Robert Carr, 1 July 1970.

the TGWU and the Amalgamated Union of Engineering and Foundry Workers (AEF), owe their position to the support of shop-floor militants and both are committed, Mr Jones of the TGWU more than Mr Scanlon of the AEF, to pursue policies which will enable shop-floor militants to make the running. In the TGWU officials are appointed by the general secretary and Mr Jones is appointing men who accept his views to key positions'. There were still, the paper noted, reliable moderate leaderships among the 'second tier' of large unions but even here 'some militants have been elected to leadership positions' and, because of the success of the TGWU, union leaders 'often find it necessary for membership reasons to adopt militant tactics themselves'.[3] For the same reasons the TUC under Vic Feather could not be relied upon to exercise a restraining influence.

The paper continued:

> the growing awareness of the power of the shop-floor and the increasing part played in wage negotiations by shop stewards have disrupted established patterns of industrial relations [...] strikes called in these circumstances are often run by unofficial committees and vulnerable to penetration by subversive influences and it is difficult for moderate union leaderships to assert control [...] there has been a considerable increase in the number of left-wing militants holding positions of influence on trade union executives and among trade union officials.

The paper provides a very fair summary of the challenges faced by the Heath government in implementing its election policy of 'bringing back order' to industrial relations. On the one hand, 'left-wing' militancy was becoming ascendant among workers themselves. On the other, trade unions, and particularly the TGWU, were changing in character, becoming more directly representative of members and facilitating far more strategic challenges to corporate leadership. It was, as the Heath government was to discover, a dangerous combination.

At the time, in summer 1970, it was the Liverpool dockers, along with Jack Dash's Royal Group in London, who were seen to be driving events. Merseyside itself provides a clear example of the longer-term changes noted at the beginning of this volume and also described by Robert Carr: the process by which shop-floor wage militancy was being transformed into a much wider 'class' movement – with growing solidarity between different groups of workers and a much more explicit political challenge to a system seen to be exploitative and unfair, a transformation reflected in the lyrics of John Lennon's song 'Imagine' (1971) – 'no need for greed or hunger, a brotherhood of man'.

---

3   TNA CAB 129/150/7, Robert Carr, 1 July 1970.

In the immediate post-war years Liverpool had been dominated by docks and shipping. It was then the main port for the US, and its 17,000 dockers handled the bulk of Britain's car exports. By the early 1970s the number of port workers was down to 10,000 – with a similar decline in the number of seafarers based at the port. Already by the late 1950s unemployment on Merseyside was well over double the British average, at 4 to 5 per cent, and far higher than that in the Midlands and the South East.[4] It was the apparent scale of this labour reserve, in Liverpool as well the North East and Scotland, that persuaded Macmillan to divert further expansion by the giant car and motor components companies out of the Midlands and the South East. The expectation was, as written into agreements with Bill Carron of the AEU and some other unions (but not the TGWU), that a major wage differential could be maintained long term.

This did not happen. Instead. the battle to equalise wages brought significant shifts in attitudes and assumptions.

Before the arrival of the new wave of car plants in the 1960s, Merseyside already possessed a number of large factories – many owned by British multinationals. Most were also some miles from the congested dockside housing in central Liverpool and sited in the new pre-war and post-war housing schemes. Dunlop tyres had been established in 1945 at Speke to the south. A number of large electrical engineering companies had been set up before the Second World War mainly in the east and north. In the 1950s these were represented by English Electric, Electric Cables and AEI. ICI had a major plant at Kirkby to the north-east along with Unilever's Birdseye factory and the BMC's Fisher Bendix factory. Five miles north-west at Netherton there was Lucas Aerospace. In some of these plants, such as ICI, BMC, Lucas and Unilever, the TGWU was already represented through deals going back to the Bevin era.[5] The TGWU also had large concentrations of membership in a number of BICC plants that then existed in the area, as well as some thousands in Yorkshire Imperial Metals, Courtaulds, Cadburys and Golden Wonder.

The new motor companies were all sited significantly further to the south of the central conurbation. British Leyland bought the land for its Speke plant, close to Dunlop, in 1959 and started production in 1961. General Motor's established its Ellesmere Port factory, far to the south-west across the Mersey, and started production in 1962. Ford's plant started production in 1963 at Halewood close to Liverpool airport, again far to the south.[6]

4 Aaron Andrews, 'Decline and the City: The Urban Crisis in Liverpool 1968–1986', PhD thesis (University of Leicester, 2018).

5 O. Sykes, J. Brown, M. Cocks, D. Shaw and C. Couch, 'A City Profile of Liverpool', *Cities*, 2013, vol.35, pp.299–318.

6 Ralph Darlington, 'Workplace Union Militancy on Merseyside since the 1960s: Extent, Nature, Causes, and Decline', *HSIR*, 2005, vol.19, no.1, pp.123–152.

While distance was undoubtedly intended to insulate the giant new factories from the militant traditions of Liverpool's waterfront (as well as, more distantly, from the wage militancy of the Midlands and South East), it seems to have offered only very temporary protection. As we saw earlier, Cousins had responded quickly in 1961 to oppose the secret union–employer deals to maintain wage differentials and later gave added support for the creation of joint shop stewards combine committees uniting plants across Britain.[7] 1962 saw the signing of an agreement by all 15 unions in engineering to secure parity across Britain by 1965 and in May 1964 Jack Jones convened a national advisory conference for the motor industry. Here he attacked the government subsidising new plants in development areas while workers were being sacked in the South East: Regions 7 (Scotland) and 12 (Merseyside) committed themselves to push forward unionisation of the new plants.[8] By 1968–1969 pay parity strikes were taking place across the BMC/Leyland plants in Lancashire and Scotland – with parallel strikes taking place in Ford Halewood and General Motors at Ellesmere Port.

In themselves, and apart from the success of the pay parity strikes, the creation of these national shop stewards combines, and the development of wage bargaining strategies at this level, marked an important step in shifting responsibilities away from the old 'Confederation' level of bargaining between unions and employers. By the 1960s shop stewards themselves were taking the initiative and in doing so, as Robert Carr noted, creating a new national shop stewards movement.

There was, however – and perhaps particularly in Liverpool – also a human element which was just as important as Len McCluskey notes in his autobiography: 'I didn't learn my politics from books [...] My politics were formed in the circumstances of the life around me life on the docks, in my trade union, and in the battles which my class fought with the establishment [...]. Much of my early political education came from talented shop stewards on the docks'.[9]

Liverpool possessed very strong traditions of independent workplace organisation in both the docks and shipping, historically its two biggest industries. In the docks the pre-Devlin structure of employment had prevented any election of firm-based representatives. Instead independent liaison committees developed spanning all firms and all dockers, whether in the TGWU or the 'Blue' stevedores union. In Liverpool, because the TGWU dock officers – as Jack Jones found in 1961 – were often far too close to the dock employers, these unofficial committees tended to see themselves as guardians of workers' rights and to be led by those

7 J. Bescoby, 'Shop Stewards Combine Committees in British Engineering', *British Journal of Industrial Relations*, 1966, vol.4, no.2, pp.154–164; Murden, 'Demands for Fair Wages'.

8 MRC MSS 126 TG/457/12, 28 May 1964.

9 Len McCluskey, *Always Red* (OR Books, 2021), pp.45–46.

politically on the Left. This was equally so among Liverpool's second biggest employer, shipping – although here the explanation was somewhat different. For almost two generations the seafarers' union leadership had operated on the far right of the Labour movement spectrum, working hand in glove with employers. This leadership was only defeated in the mid-1960s. Again, over many decades, unofficial liaison committees had operated. Their main base was in Liverpool.

The leaders needed to be people of strong commitment. Those organising the three national (unofficial) seafarers' strikes prior to 1966 had all suffered arrest and imprisonment during those earlier conflicts. In 1966 one leader was Joe Kenny, a Communist Party member who worked closely with the local MP Eric Heffer and was denounced by Wilson in the Commons. Another was Jack Coward, like Jack Jones a veteran of the Spanish Civil War (wounded and for a time a Franco prisoner), who had been to the fore in most working-class struggles in Liverpool since the 1930s. Both had been organisers of the Seaman's Reform Movement and its journal the *Seaman's Charter*. Another younger leader was David Thompson, also arrested previously. Among the dockers' unofficial leaders was another veteran of the Spanish war, Frank Deegan, TGWU member and personally recruited by Jack Jones to serve in Spain in 1937. Others include Denis Kelly, originally a communist, and Ben Bow, a leader of the 'Blue' union.

These unofficial leaders had a political perspective that was deeply rooted in past struggles, saw the need to create a new society free from exploitation and sought to apply the lessons of past struggles to the present. Elsewhere in Liverpool were those with similar commitments. Bill Jones was convener in the city's direct works department, chair of the Merseyside Joint Union Committee and key figure in the Building Workers Charter. Stan Pemberton was a key activist within the TGWU, a steward at the Dunlop Rubber Speke factory throughout his working life and later chair of the TGWU's General Executive Council. Across the Mersey in the Cammel Laird shipyard was Barry Williams, chair of the boilermakers' area committee and president of Liverpool Trades Council. Down at General Motors at Ellesmere Port a young Tony Woodley was already a shop steward. All were either on the Left of the Labour Party or communists and around them were hundreds of other activists who – to a greater or less degree – shared the same perspectives.

As jobs in the docks were lost and, as the new workplaces opened, significant numbers of dockers ended up in the car plants or finding jobs in the earlier generation of new factories such as Dunlop, Fisher Bendix, Lucas or AEI. And as unemployment temporarily declined through the 1960s they ensured that the opportunity was used to push up local wage levels that had remained far below the national average.

Ford came up to Merseyside with every intention of maintaining the differential. Eddie Roberts, later a regional TGWU officer, remembers applying for a job in 1962 after being made redundant at Dunlop. He was just married. The recruitment officer at Ford was only interested in married men with family commitments, hire purchase and preferably a mortgage – guarantees, it was thought, of a workforce that would not strike. Yet this did not happen at Ford Halewood. Workers like Eddie Roberts, already an active trade unionist at Dunlop, brought with them experience of trade union militancy elsewhere, ensured that the workforce was organised and within a few years had enforced pay parity.[10]

This was the background to Merseyside's very high levels of strike action in the 1960s and also to its remarkable record of solidarity between different groups of workers, solidarity organised and consolidated by Liverpool Trades Council and the Merseyside Joint Union Committee. The ten-week bus strike in 1968 was in part sustained by solidarity contributions from 50,000 other Liverpool workers. The following year the attempted occupation of Merseyside's electronic factories – to halt closures in face of the General Electric Company (GEC) amalgamation – was similarly sustained by workplace donations elsewhere. Tony McQuade, a panel beater originally from Scotland Road with a seaman father, secured a job at the new British Leyland factory which quickly became the highest paid factory in the area. But it was also renowned for its solidarity – striking to support both nurses and also the dockers when they struck work to ensure that foreign crews were paid their wages. Under the leadership of Bobby Owens, the shop stewards committee at Leyland insisted on the management recruiting, as a matter of policy, those from black and ethnic minorities and a regular percentage of those with disabilities. In 1973–1974 Chilean refugees were also found work.[11]

This ethic of working-class solidarity ensured that in Liverpool, as we saw earlier, the impact of containerisation was successfully limited by an agreement between dockers and road haulage workers.[12] It was *joint* industrial action, of dockers and drivers combined, that forced compliance by employers – in sharp contrast to London.

This contrast was equally true for white-collar trade unionism. In the early 1970s Liverpool registered a particularly sharp shift towards a trade union (and working-class) identity among the previously largely non-union clerical and managerial workers in the docks. In the 1960s the TGWU Association of Clerical, Technical and Supervisory Staff (ACTSS) clerical branch 5/567 had only a few dozen members. By 1972 it had grown to 300 and by 1974 to 800. By then it represented virtually 100 per cent of white-collar staff in the Mersey Harbour Dock Company. The big shift to

10 Eddie Roberts, interview by John Foster, 2020, Unite Oral History Archive.

11 Tony McQuade, interview by John Foster, 2020, Unite Oral History Archive.

12 G. Taylor, 'From "Unofficial Militants" to *De Facto* Joint Workplace Control: The Development of the Shop Steward System at the Port of Liverpool, 1967–1972', *Labour History*, 2017, vol.58, no.4, pp.552–575

100 per cent membership followed a month's strike by white-collar workers across the Mersey docks. This strike, backed by solidarity action by registered dock workers, was called to halt redundancies of clerical staff in the process of Liverpool's dock modernisation and rationalisation. It coincided with the nationwide Pentonville Five strike but continued three weeks beyond it and eventually compelled the dock company to maintain the employment of virtually all those previously threatened with redundancy. Further industrial action by the ACTSS branch in 1973 successfully maintained wage levels in face of double-digit inflation. The TGWU officer responsible was Eddie Roberts, previously convener at Fords Halewood, and one of the ACTSS shop stewards was a young Len McClusky.[13]

Nor was this type of solidarity limited to the workplace. When Liverpool's council tenants resisted rent increases under the Tory's Housing Finance Act in 1973, the imprisonment of tenants resulted in a local one-day General Strike led by dockers and building workers. However, back in July 1970, as Robert Carr and his departmental officials compiled in their Cabinet brief, it would have been the local strength of the LCDTU that was foremost in their minds. This had ensured that Merseyside had consistently supported its calls for strike action in 1969 and 1970 against *In Place of Strife* [14] – and would do so again in 1971 and 1972.

The Heath Government: Unable to Govern in the Old Way

The Conservative Party came into office in the summer of 1970 with a wide ranging and somewhat contradictory programme that in part reflected the conflicting views within the Conservative Party and the new Cabinet.

Some members, Keith Joseph, Nicholas Ridley, Maurice Macmillan and Margaret Thatcher, wanted a decisive change of direction. They saw the post-war cross-party commitment to full employment and a universal welfare state as enabling the development of a far too confident and challenging working class. In response they urged the discipline of significantly higher unemployment, the cutting back of state expenditure and particularly an end to the universalist principles of the welfare state. They prioritised legislation on benefits, social insurance, council house rents, a return to means testing and the ending of subsidies to failing firms and Britain's regions.

Others like John Davies, until a few weeks before general secretary of the CBI and now Industry Minister, carried forward the more immediate

---

13 Eddie Roberts, interview by John Foster, 2020; G. Taylor, 'White-Collar Workers and Industrial Militancy: The Formation of the ACTSS 6/567 Branch at the Port of Liverpool', *Labour History Review*, 2016, vol.81, no.3, pp.49–75; G. Taylor, 'Internecine Strife in Trade Union Organisations', *Labor History*, 2018, vol.59, no.2, pp.162–184.
14 Industrial Relations White Paper, 'In Place of Strife', Cmnd 3888.

priorities of big business: a reduction of state expenditure and measures to curb wage militancy. Heath himself, together with his principal associates – the new chancellor Anthony Barber, Peter Walker at Environment, Reginald Maudling at the Board of Trade and Robert Carr – wanted to maintain the main elements of the post-war settlement, continue the modernisation of the economy, create a legal framework for restoring moderate leadership to the trade union movement and, most critical of all, take Britain into the EEC so that, to quote Heath, Britain could become its leading financial and banking centre.[15]

Initially, however, there was a measure of unity. Priorities were identified as the need to reduce state expenditure, to press forward negotiations for EEC membership – now feasible after the resignation of De Gaulle – and to provide a new legislative framework for labour relations sustained by the rhetoric of curbing inflationary wage pressures and protecting the poor and those on fixed incomes.

However, within little less than 15 months, by October 1971, this programme was in serious trouble. An assessment by the Central Policy Review Staff, run by Heath's ally Lord Rothschild, concluded that, with the exception of EEC negotiations, there had been very limited progress and that a number of policies were going badly awry.[16] Unemployment had not checked inflation. 'Even when taken to the limits of what is politically acceptable [it] provides no adequate check on excessive price and cost increases'.[17] On the contrary, the sharp increase in unemployment over the year, already rising towards the million mark, had resulted in a significant increase in public expenditure on benefits. The cuts in funding to nationalised industries, such as coal, power and steel, had forced up prices to the private sector. The withdrawal of support from Rolls Royce and UCS had had even worse results. Campaigns for their rescue united working-class communities in opposition and, in the regions affected, eroded the Conservative Party's traditional small business base, in turn damaging support for the government's flagship Industrial Relations Act.

In assessing why the 1971 TUC had voted for non-cooperation, requiring unions to refuse to register under the legal terms of the Act, Rothschild's report singled out the 'UCS factor'. Although the legislation had now become law, 'extreme militancy has become more rather than less evident than it was fifteen months ago'. Almost twice the number of days had been lost through industrial action than in the same period the previous year. The report continued 'experience of the last two years

15 TNA 129/158/24, Heath to Cabinet, 30 September1971, Review of government strategy 10 (i).

16 TNA CAB 129/159/4, Burke Trend, 30 September 1971.

17 TNA CAB 129/159/4, Burke Trend, 30 September 1971.

suggests that legislation exacerbates rather than improves the situation, at least in the short run' and goes on to note 'the increasing power within the trade union movement of left-wing militancy – often operating at shop-floor level in defiance of union executives'. In October 1971, as Heath prepared to demote two of his most right-wing ministers, he summed up the report by remarking that the government had been seen to be 'hard-hearted rather than hard-headed'.[18]

However, this reversal of policy on industrial support and unemployment – later to be described as Heath's U-turn – did little to overcome the underlying problems. These were largely beyond Heath's control and stemmed from long-term changes in the balance of power within the global economy.

In 1971–1972 the post-war system of currency control and IMF-manipulated debts, the basis of the Anglo-American grip over Third World economies, had finally broken apart. For three decades this system had enabled the western powers to extract cheap oil, food stuffs and minerals from the ex-colonial world. This had been very profitable for the companies which controlled their sale – including British multinationals such as BP, Shell and Unilever. But it led to the increasing impoverishment of their producers.

Now popular movements in previously subordinate countries were challenging this external control. Chile moved to nationalise copper in 1971 and led the way in establishing a copper producers' cartel. In 1971 Algeria and Libya also nationalised oil and the Organisation of Petroleum Exporting States (OPEC), which included the main Middle Eastern oil producers, enforced a 60 per cent increase in the price of oil. The global price of basic food stuffs also rose sharply. Then in August of 1971, and largely because of the costs of the Vietnam War, the United States, with its gold reserves almost exhausted, abandoned the gold-dollar link – the cornerstone of the post-war currency system – and devalued the dollar first by 10 per cent and then another 6 per cent. Inflationary pressures, largely stemming from OPEC's control over oil supplies, then escalated further in 1972–1973. Annual inflation in Britain increased from 6 per cent in 1970 to 9 per cent in 1971 and just under 16 per cent by 1974. The profitability of British companies, hitherto significantly dependent on overseas earnings, also fell sharply – from 10 per cent in 1969 to 8 per cent for 1970 to 1972 and 4 per cent by 1974.[19]

These were the underlying factors that made it impossible for Heath to govern in the old way – even though for the next three years he attempted to do so.

18 TNA CAB 129/159/6, Heath to Cabinet, 5 October 1971.
19 Middlemas, *Power, Competition and the State: Threats*, pp.341–348.

Work-Ins, Occupations and Action Committees

Conference instructs that where Action Committees are set up to assist in the promotion of opposition to factory closures, rent increases, unfair legislation and to assist old age pensioners claims, they will have full support of the union and its officers (MRC MSS 126/ TG/1887/25, 1973 Biennial Conference, minute 18).

This resolution was passed unanimously at the TGWU's July 1973 biennial conference. It reflected the degree to which a much more self-confident working-class movement was emerging in the early 1970s, one that sought to encompass, at local community level, all sections of working people and where mutual solidarity between different groups was becoming the norm. Usually these action committees were formed, as they had been previously in the 1920s, around local trades councils. Sometimes they sprang directly from the struggles of local workplaces to resist closure. Many were established across the summer and autumn of 1971 to organise local backing and financial collections for the first and biggest of the occupations/work-ins, that at UCS. The UCS stewards sent committee members systematically across the country to broaden political support and secure the wages needed to sustain the work-in and maintain, for the following 15 months, the defiant challenge of the 8,000 workers on the Clyde.

The TGWU played a significant part in mobilising this wider support. Although it had relatively few workers in the Clyde shipyards themselves, it did play a crucial role in building the movement across Britain. Two TGWU officers were particularly important. The Scottish regional secretary, Ray MacDonald, was in 1971–1972 president of the Scottish Trade Union Congress (STUC) and in that capacity flew down to London with leading stewards for the parliamentary debate on the Monday after the closure crisis broke. He also, along with STUC staff, helped organise the public enquiry in September 1972 that shifted Scottish opinion, particularly among the business community, against the government. Equally important was his role in the Scottish Assembly convened by the STUC in February 1972.

The other officer was Hugh Wyper, MacDonald's successor as Scottish secretary of the TGWU. Wyper, acting as an officer for the Confed, played a key role from the Left in UCS negotiations and was present at the famous meeting between UCS stewards and government ministers on 29 September 1971 when the government's U-turn began – conceding support for three of the four previously doomed yards.

Over a hundred occupation and work-ins took place over the following 12 months (A. J. Mills, 'Worker Occupations, 1971–1975: A Sociohistorical Analysis of the Development and Spread of Sit-Ins, Work-Ins and Worker

Co-Operative in Britain', PhD thesis, Durham, 1982, http://etheses.dur.
ac.uk/7406/). Many were relatively short. Some, especially in the North West
in 1972–1973, were over issues of pay, e.g. when the Engineering Employers
Federation sought a showdown with militant shop stewards and workers
responded by occupying.

A significant number, however, were, like the UCS, against closure. The most
emblematic of these was probably that at Briant Colour Printing in Bermondsey.
This was also a work-in. The printworks were in Old Kent Road in the heart of
working-class south London only two or three miles from the docks. A major
and highly efficient print supplier, Briant's had around 130 employees and been
operating for almost a century. In 1971 it changed hands and the following
year, on 21 June 1972, the Joint Chapel Committee were summoned to a
meeting and told the company had gone into liquidation. The firm had a strong
order book – and there was no prior warning. The stewards, when informed
that the plant would close, immediately called a meeting of the workforce and
secured a unanimous decision to work-in – to secure the building and continue
production (Dennis McGrath, *The Right to Work: Briant Colour Printing Work-In*.
Foreword by Tony Benn, BCP Work-In Committee 2002).

The workforce belonged to a range of print and design unions, the Society
of Graphical and Allied Trades (SOGAT), National Society of Operative Printers
and Assistances (NATSOPA), National Graphical Association (NGA) and the
Society of Lithographic Artists and Engravers (SLADE), all of which gave official
backing to the work-in and provided some continuing financial support. The
workers soon found that most commercial orders had been shifted to other
companies. However, orders quickly came in from trade unions, shop stewards
committees and Ruskin College in Oxford.

Chrissie Brazil was Mother of Chapel and remembers the strength of
local support from Bermondsey and neighbouring working-class communities. Chrissie Brazil had joined the firm the previous year, still an apprentice,
moving from a printers in Westminster to be closer to Bermondsey where her
family lived. All were dockers, TGWU members. 'Every day people came in to
offer help'. Weekly rallies were held with speakers from the London unions, the
local trades council and from UCS to which Briant's workers had previously
sent collections (Christine Brazil, 1972 BCP Mother of Chapel/Chair of the
Joint Union Committee, interview by John Foster, 13 February 2021, Unite Oral
History Archive).

Four weeks into the work-in the Pentonville Five were arrested. It was from
the Briant Colour fundraising rally on Saturday 22 July on Clerkenwell Green
that the chair of the liaison committee made the first call for general strike
action. From that moment the Briant Colour workers were printing non-stop
the thousands of posters and leaflets used to publicise the call – so much so
that accusations of 'conspiracy' were levelled at them in the Commons. The
following month the dockers returned their support. The Briant workers had

started to picket the local paper supply firm whose debts had been used to trigger the liquidation. On the picket they were met with brutal treatment and arrests by the Special Patrol Group, a unit especially established by the government for use against workers' protests. Dockers, led by Bernie Steer and Vic Turner, came in to offer support.

The work-in continued for a further year until a buyer was found. It was, said Chrissie Brazil, remarkably united with no wavering. Women workers, 25 in all, played an important role in the leadership, travelling to other workplaces to win support. Chrissie herself remembers travelling to Shotton steel works in South Wales. Bill Freeman, the convener and a member of the LCDTU's organising committee, worked to keep the work-in at the centre of the movement's concerns.

It was such examples of wider class solidarity that would have been in the minds of the TGWU's conference delegates in the summer of 1973 when they passed the motion of full support for action committees – to oppose factory closures, rent increases and to support pensioners against poverty.

The TGWU and Resistance to the Anti-union Offensive

In leading resistance to the government's attack on trade union rights and living standards Jack Jones demonstrated the same strategic understanding as Frank Cousins. He made it his job to expose the central assumption of the government's propaganda: that increases in prices were caused by wage rises. On the contrary, those to blame were the companies who actually set the prices: monopolies exploiting their market power to offset losses overseas by gouging income out of consumers in Britain.

At the September 1970 Labour Party conference Jones highlighted the resulting plight of the low paid and particularly pensioners, and won support for a mass campaign to publicise pensioner poverty. At the same conference, using the same arguments, he won support, against the platform, for resistance to any form of wage restraint.[20] Then in October 1970, when the Tory government's anti-union legislation was published. Jack Jones, along with Hugh Scanlon was able to win the TUC General Council for a campaign of active opposition.[21] A mass rally was held in the Albert Hall on 12 January 1971 accompanied by some strike action organised by the LCDTU. A mass demonstration was held on 21 February attended by up to 200,000, probably the biggest demonstration in London since the 1920s and again followed by further strikes called by the LCDTU.

20 Jones, *Union Man*, pp.227.
21 Jones, *Union Man*, pp.229–231.

In March 1971 the TUC held a special conference in Croydon. Here Jones and Scanlon were less successful. They failed to win support for industrial action against the new legislation. Instead, there was a more limited agreement that unions should seek to make the new legislation ineffective, particularly by ensuring that in future wage negotiations agreements should not be legally binding. In this way unofficial strikes could not be used under the new Act to fine unions for breach of contract.[22]

It was at this point that the broader campaign of opposition also faltered. With unemployment rising rapidly, calls by the LCDTU for new strikes for May–June 1971 failed to find widespread support. As we have seen, what appears to have transformed the situation was the work-in on the Clyde and the deepening crisis of political control confronting the government across July, August and September 1971. When Lord Rothschild cited the 'UCS factor' to explain the victory for Jones and Scanlon at the 1971 TUC, he was indicating not just a local struggle on the Clyde but the way it had transformed attitudes across the country – giving a common focus to hundreds of local struggles on workers' rights and unemployment. The all-Britain shop stewards meeting called by the UCS stewards in August 1971, attended by 1,500, and the two one-day mass political strikes in Scotland in July and August 1971, brought a new awareness of a common strength. It was also this rank-and-file mobilisation that gave courage to the 100 subsequent workplace occupations and produced a renewed determination to defy the Industrial Relations Act at the TUC Congress in September.[23]

However, still in early December 1971, and probably in light of Heath's reversal of policy on regional economic support, Robert Carr at Employment believed there remained hope for the ultimate success of the Industrial Relations Act. It was, he wrote, 'premature' to assess how far the boycott would impede reforms. Although, he wrote, there was no significant move among the unions to break ranks, he believed that among the white-collar unions inter-union competition might bring this about.[24]

At this point, on 1 December, Carr seems to have had no inkling that the next blow against the government's programme would come in just four weeks' time and that it would be delivered by the miners, largely dismissed as a threat in his July 1970 survey.

The Coal Board had refused to give serious consideration to the miners' demand for an increase that would recompense them for the major fall in income during the previous decade of contraction. On 9 January 1972 they embarked on a national strike, the first official miners' strike since 1926. The government seem to have relied on the existence of large

22 Seifert and Sibley, *Revolutionary Communist*, pp.178–181.
23 Jones, *Union Man*, pp.232–233; C. Woolfson, *The UCS Work-in* (Lawrence and Wishart, 1986), chapter 6.
24 TNA CAB 129/160/12, Carr, 1 December 1971.

stocks of coal, coke and oil and failed to anticipate the scale of solidarity that would be forthcoming from other workers.

The role of the TGWU was crucial. In his autobiography Jack Jones notes: 'Ray Buckton of ASLEF and I were determined to do all we could to offer support. I told Joe Gormley [of the miners] that if you want to stop oil going into the power stations you'll have to get your men to picket them'.[25] Pickets enabled the drivers of commercial haulage, tankers and trains to turn back with legal protection. Jack Jones himself attended the picket lines to reinforce the message. Most supplies were halted.

However, by early February it became clear that some non-union commercial haulage drivers were continuing to move fuel from the giant Midlands coke depot at Saltley Gate. On 10 February the TGWU and fellow trade unionists in Birmingham mobilised the factories. Faced with thousands of pickets, and large numbers of arrests, the police closed the gates – marking the beginning of the end for the government's resistance. A commission of enquiry was then appointed under Lord Wilberforce who found in favour of the miners' claim and by the end of February had recommended a 27 per cent rise. Inter-union solidarity had been key. As Jack Jones remarked, it finally made up for 'the betrayal of 1926'.[26]

Directly arising from the miners' strike, and the failure of the Department of Employment to give adequate warning, a new department of Cabinet was created to plan against future emergencies: the COBR committee.[27]

On 22 February, in response to this new setback, Robert Carr produced a report for the Cabinet that listed in detail anticipated or possible public sector strikes over the following three months. For each he assessed the likely 'economic power' that could be marshalled by the unions. The London bus workers were not seen to represent a major threat. A strike by postal workers would be 'highly disruptive' but only serious if joined or supported by the post officers engineers. The teachers would 'not be very damaging'. Nurses would, however, be able to wield some 'political power'. Hospital electricians would constitute a problem if the strike continued for more than four weeks. A strike by airline ground staff would be damaging but fall short of a full emergency unless supported by other airport workers. The likely action by rail workers was dangerous. The Associated Society of Locomotive Engineers and Firemen (ASLEF) was more militant than the National Union of Railwaymen (NUR) and coal and fuel stocks had not recovered from the coal strike. Emergency powers might be required. In steel, strike action could have a widespread impact on industry if stocks were not built up.

25 Jones, *Union Man*, p.245.
26 Jones, *Union Man*, pp.244–245.
27 TNA CAB 129/161/18, Lord Rothschild, 14 February 1972.

Carr added that in the private sector there was a range of pay demands pending in the large engineering companies and that he was urging the need to restrict agreements to 8 per cent (inflation was then running at something over 8 per cent).

However, Carr's report once more failed to notice the most obvious danger. This was the continuing dispute in the docks over containerisation. In just over four months' time, the issue of containerisation would trigger a General Strike which would finally sink the Tory government's Industrial Relations Act.[28] This story will be told in the final chapter. Next, however, we will look at another key factor making for this victory: the growing strength of the TGWU numerically and, no less important, politically.

Strengthening the Union: Strengthening the Left

March 1971 saw the first of a series of major mergers that strengthened both the union and the Left within it. In March 1971 the 20,000 strong Scottish Commercial Motormen voted by six to one to join the TGWU. Its general secretary Alex Kitson was a strong Left-winger. He noted that bringing together the two major unions in commercial transport in Scotland was 'a necessary first step before we begin the task of organising the unorganised' with the aim of wiping out 'non-unionism completely in the industry in Scotland'.[29] Kitson became the union's deputy general secretary. Before the merger the TGWU had already announced an increase in membership over the previous year of 107,000 – bringing the total to 1,638,000, the biggest increase in membership ever. A quarter of it, a sign of times, was in the salaried staff sector.[30]

Six months later, in September, two more unions joined. From Thames there was the historic Watermen's, Lightermen's and Bargemen's Union, founded in 1871, helping to complete the TGWU's dominance in the Port of London. At the same time the strongly left-wing Chemical Workers Union joined. This brought another 30,000 members, many of them in ICI. Its general secretary, Bob Edwards MP, commented 'we live in an era of class struggle and in this struggle, particularly in the chemical industry, organised workers have to confront the concentrated power of the some of the largest and most powerful monopolies'. The TGWU under Cousins and Jones 'had evolved into a general industrial union [...] which gave voice to rank and file workers' to make the TGWU 'a progressive socialist force'.[31]

Then finally in December 1971 the NUVB brought in another 83,000 members with a four to one majority in favour. This went a long way to

28 TNA CAB 129/161/22, Robert Carr to Cabinet, 22 February 1972.
29 TGWU *Record*, March 1971.
30 TGWU *Record*, March 1971.
31 TGWU *Record*, November 1971.

Figure 4: Jack Jones, Alex Kitson, Michael Foot and Harry Urwin
(from Irene Kitson)

create a single industrial union for motor manufacturing with 70 per cent
of the workforce in membership in Britain and over 90 per cent in Ireland.
Its acting general secretary Grenville Hawley became secretary of the
new motor manufacturing trade group. This merger, wrote Jack Jones,
'consolidated the progress we made in engineering with the full merger
with the National Union of Enginemen, Mechanics and Electrical Workers
and with the Process and General Workers in chemicals'.[32] The process
was completed the following year with the return of the Scottish TGWU,
covering dockers in the Clyde estuary and a number of other Scottish
ports, who had broken away 40 years before in 1932 in protest at the
policies of the union under Ernest Bevin.[33]

　　The union's 1971 biennial conference marked the growing strength
of the Left. Delegates demanded complete non-cooperation with the
Industrial Relations Act. They called on the TGWU to 'use all its
authority to demand affiliated unions of the TUC, and impress on other

---

32　TGWU *Record*, December 1971.
33　A. Murray, *The T&G Story* (Lawrence and Wishart, 2008), p.161.

unions, the need for a sustained policy of non-cooperation [...] and to take the strongest possible action should sanctions be imposed'. They also referred back to 'the damage done to the Labour Party and the Trade Union Movement arising from the previous Labour government's White Paper 'In Place of Strike' and asked for both the Labour Party NEC and the Parliamentary Labour Party to give an explicit and unconditional assurance for the repeal of the Industrial Relations legislation'.[34] This motion was moved with the support of 16 branches from London and East, ten from Merseyside and the North West, seven from the Midlands and a scattering from elsewhere. There was also unanimous support for the call for the next Labour government to carry through the socialist principles of Clause 4. A motion of opposition to the Conservative plans for joining the EEC was passed 'overwhelmingly' with resolutions in support from London, the Midlands, Scotland and Ireland.[35]

The 1971 conference also strengthened policy on key international issues, calling for moves to overcome Cold War divisions within Europe and the international trade union movement and enhancing the union's role of solidarity with international struggles for democracy and liberation. Resolutions were carried calling for the recognition of the German Democratic Republic (GDR), opposing the US war in Vietnam, particularly its extension to Cambodia and Laos, and also demanding an end to arms sales to South Africa.[36]

The pages of the TGWU *Record* for 1971–1972 reflected this agenda of active engagement. The most featured stories were those describing current industrial struggles: the strike over trade union rights at the US-owned Fine Tubes in Plymouth entering its second year; victory across the Ford combine with a 16.5 per cent pay increase; women flax and hemp workers on strike throughout Fife for a living wage and, recurring for the next 12 months, the work-in by the UCS workers.[37] The campaign against the Industrial Relations Act continued – with constant reminders of the need to rebut government propaganda linking inflation to wage increases. The causation, the *Record* argued, was the other way around. It was inflation itself that forced workers to push wage demands. The *Record* also focused on why membership of the EEC would lead to the progressive erosion of Britain's industrial economy. Internationally, the *Record* highlighted campaigns of solidarity with trade unionists in fascist Spain and Portugal and on developing closer relations with the socialist countries – with reports of exchanges with Soviet trade unionists and visits to Poland, the GDR and Romania.

34 MRC MSS 126/TG/1887/24, 1971 Biennial Conference, minute 37.
35 MRC MSS 126/TG/1887/24, 1971 Biennial Conference, minute 39.
36 MRC MSS 126/TG/1887/24, 1971 Biennial Conference, minute 45 and 65.
37 TGWU *Record*, July 1971.

The TGWU biennial conference for 1973 also began to look ahead to another general election and a potential Labour victory. It demonstrated the membership's determination to sustain the perspectives for socialist transformation originally laid out by Frank Cousins in 1960 but now far more explicitly. Labour must not return to the wage policies of the previous Wilson government. A composite motion calling for the union to 'continue policies to avoid a wages free for all' was defeated. Instead conference passed a composite moved by Eric Rechnitz calling for 'unfettered collective bargaining'. 'The undue emphasis placed upon wage levels being a major source of inflationary pressure has now been totally disproved'.[38] Conference also deepened its commitment to public ownership. 'Where the economy requires the creation of large units of production, services etc they should be taken into public ownership and should provide for genuine participation in management by workers'.[39]

Conference went on to deplore the 'gift of 80 per cent of the North Sea's hydrocarbon wealth to the private multinationals' and called 'for immediate nationalisation under workers and community control of North Sea and Irish Sea exploration, production, transportation and distribution with compensation only for actual expenditure incurred'. In the face of attempts to define worker participation in ways that would constrain trade union freedom conference 'welcomed steps by unions to extend the participation of members in the control of wages and conditions and of industry in general' and reaffirmed support for the extension of industrial democracy' with representatives on management and supervisory boards 'without any loss of freedom or autonomy as trade union members'.[40]

Conference also sought to define a new and far more active and member-led relationship to the Labour Party. Conference carried 'overwhelmingly' a motion from branches in South East, Wales and the Midlands urging the executive to 'encourage members to be active in the Labour Party' and 'to work for a Labour Party pledged to socialist ideals that will fight for the trade union movement [...] involving the shop-floor membership in plants, factories and industry in general in the affairs and policy making of the Labour Party' and considers that 'the constitution of the Labour Party should be amended to allow for membership of factory branches with ward status'.[41] At the same time conference also gave unanimous support for a motion calling for a widening of union campaigning into communities.[42] On the issue of the EEC, conference rejected a motion calling for the union to take places on EEC committees

38 MRC MSS 126/TG/1887/25, 1973 Biennial Conference, minute 20.
39 MRC MSS 126/TG/1887/25. Minutes and Record of the 25th Biennial Delegate Conference, July 1973.
40 MRC MSS 126/TG/1887/25, 1973 Biennial Conference minutes.
41 MRC MSS 126/TG/1887/25, 1973 Biennial Conference, minute 50.
42 MRC MSS 126/TG/1887/25, 1973 Biennial Conference, minute 18.

and passed a motion demanding a referendum on EEC membership.[43] On European security conference called unanimously for the recognition of the GDR and the establishment of nuclear free zones.

Over the same year the TGWU *Record* details the implementation of these international commitments. The union protested at the visit to Britain of Portugal's fascist leader Caetano and at the same time formed an 'international' branch of the union for Portuguese workers in Britain, many of them political refugees. It also called for support for the 300 trade unionists and democrats still in prison in Greece following the US-backed military coup of 1967.[44] In August Jack Jones reported on the TUC delegation to meet Soviet trade unionists in Moscow: 'British-Soviet trade union relations are moving towards the situation that existed in the last war'.[45]

In November 1973 Jones reported on another international TUC visit jointly with Vic Feather – this time to South Africa. This was far more problematic. On the Left there was some disquiet about any visit to apartheid South Africa. At the same time, within the TUC itself there were some unions which still opposed any active policy of boycott and tended, on the grounds of protecting jobs, to support the Conservative government's policy of maintaining active economic relations with South Africa. In his autobiography Jack Jones describes his efforts to make contact with British activists imprisoned in apartheid jails as well as his success in thwarting Vic Feather's plan to secure an anodyne final press statement. Instead Jones himself drafted a forthright condemnation of apartheid which called for the political and economic liberation of the black population.[46] Another key area of solidarity was with the workers of Chile after the September 1973 coup, a cause with which, as we will see, Jack Jones closely identified.

Nearer to home, in Ireland, the TGWU faced a far more direct challenge to its values of working-class solidarity. In June 1972 Jack Jones's report to the executive had called for a speedy political initiative to avert 'the drift towards civil war' and called for the end to internment without trial and the transfer of responsibilities for security to Westminster. The union's biennial conference in July 1973 noted the further deterioration and 'paid tribute to officers, active trade unionists and all concerned who, despite the many difficulties, had succeeded in maintaining stability in the offices, factories and workshops. This was a notable achievement'.[47] In some ways it was indeed one of the most important (and difficult) achievements of the TGWU in this period and we will examine it in the next chapter.

43 MRC MSS 126/TG/1887/25, 1973 Biennial Conference, minute 39.
44 TGWU *Record*, May 1973.
45 TGWU *Record*, August 1973.
46 TGWU *Record*, November 1973; Jones, *Union Man*, pp.274–275.
47 MRC MSS 126/TG/1186/A/50, TGWU GEC 8 June 1972. Appendix 1, General Secretary's Quarterly Report; MRC MSS 126/TG/1887/25, 1973 Biennial Conference, minute 39.

Solidarity with Chilean Democrats

On 12 September 1973 Bobby Somerville, senior shop steward at Rolls Royce East Kilbride, watched on television as Hawker Hunter jets, powered by Rolls Royce engines, demolished the presidential palace in Santiago, Chile. Two days later, on Friday 14 September, he moved a resolution at the plant's Joint Shop Stewards Committee condemning the fascist coup and pledging solidarity with all those in Chile resisting the new dictatorship. The resolution was passed unanimously by a Committee with delegates from the Amalgamated Union of Engineering Workers (AEUW), TGWU and a number of smaller craft unions representing the 3,000 strong workforce. This account is based on interviews by John Foster with Yvonne Strachan (August 2020), Robert Somerville (October 2020), Jane McKay (October 2020), Irene Kitson (November 2020) and statements from Bobby Starrett and Tom Morrison, the film 'Nae Pasaran' released in 2018 (Felipe Bustos Sierra) and Ann Jones, *No Truck with the Chilean Junta: Trade Union Internationalism 1973–1980* (Canberra, 2014).

Just days before, at the 1973 Trade Union Congress, Jack Jones had warned of the perilous situation in Chile. He likened it to that in Spain just before the invasion by Franco's Army of Africa. A month later, in the TGWU *Record* for October, he wrote: 'all progressive opinion must strongly deplore the actions of the military attacking the democratic government of Chile which has led to the death of President Allende [...] we are at the beginning of another Spanish war situation [...]. These developments should strengthen the determination of all trade unionists to be vigilant in resisting the attacks of fascists and big business' (TGWU *Record*, October 1973). We now know that the coup was orchestrated by the United States' Central Intelligence Agency fearful of another Cuba in the Americas and the loss of Chile's precious copper reserves (Lubna Quereshi, *Nixon, Kissinger and Allende: US Involvement in the Coup in 1973*, Lexington Books 2008).

What was known at the time was that many Chilean trade unionists had been killed and Britain's government had recognised the US-backed coup regime. The November issues of the TGWU *Record* reported that 'TGWU members have been extremely active in protesting about the government's recognition of the Chilean Junta [...] dockers have been reported as unwilling to handle military goods bound for Chile' (TGWU *Record*, November 1973). Alex Kitson, as newly appointed deputy general secretary of the TGWU, had been to the fore contacting officers of the TGWU in his native Scotland – including the district officer Hugh Wyper and Jane McKay of the TGWU Scottish Women's Committee. That November the TGWU Scottish Women's Committee forwarded a motion to the STUC Women's Advisory Committee calling for a campaign of solidarity action – a motion that opened the way to a much broader movement of support in Scotland, one taken up by the STUC and its deputy general secretary at the time, Jimmy Milne. Glasgow was a city that had sent many volunteers to fight in Spain. Jane remembers her mother saying: 'This is another Spain'. 'People opened their hearts to the refugees'.

Initially this support was for political prisoners still in Chilean prisons and then, increasingly, as refugee families began to arrive in Britain, the provision of housing, material support and assistance with education and employment. In 1974 the Scottish Chile Defence Committee was set up with TGWU member Joe Frame as secretary, AUEW Glasgow secretary Alex Ferry as chair and Jane McKay, also TGWU, as treasurer. It was backed by trade unions and trades councils from across Scotland. From Ayrshire through to Clydebank and Fife, Aberdeen to Dumfries, local councils were won to provide housing. Word was spread on the need for all kinds of house furnishings and an overwhelming response was received from the labour and trade union movement and people in the communities. Jane McKay also remembers one political prisoner, adopted in Scotland, saying, when he finally arrived in Scotland, how much the letters and postcards had meant to him when imprisoned in Chile.

East Kilbride (and Lanarkshire more generally) was typical of this wider solidarity – with local MPs, Judith Hart and Jeremy Bray (Motherwell and Wishaw), working with local trades councils to ensure that local councils and housing authorities provided support. Many trade unionists, including Bobby Somerville, provided temporary accommodation. So did many other local community organisations including local churches. Bobby remembers that none of the refugees wanted to talk about what happened to them. One who was badly tortured and had his legs broken only spoke about his treatment in prison many years later.

Arising from this depth of local community support and knowledge, it was not surprising that an engineer working in the refit shop, Bob Fulton, hitherto 'non-political' and a church warden, approached Bobby Somerville in March 1974 to say he was refusing to work on an aeroengine. He believed it to be from Chile. Somerville soon checked and found it was one of eight engines sent for repair from the self-same Hawker Hunter jets that had strafed the presidential palace seven months before.

On the basis of the resolution passed the previous September, the JSSC immediately gave support to a boycott of the engines, and on 23 March 1974 sent a request for support to the AEUW executive and to Tony Benn, as minister in the newly elected Labour government. The May meeting of the AEUW executive passed a resolution to boycott all Chilean military work across Britain while the Parliamentary Labour Party Defence and Overseas Policy Committee called on the government to cancel all Chilean military contracts (MRC MSS 126/TG/1186/A/51, TGWU GEC 19 September 1973 and 5 December 1973 and MRC MSS 126/TG/1186/A/52, GEC 7 June 1974; TNA CAB 129/176/6, Benn to Cabinet calling for cancellation of contracts with Chile

26 April 1974; CAB 129/176/7, Callaghan to Cabinet, 29 April 1974 with report from British ambassador in Washington).

It was at this point that the pro-US foreign secretary James Callaghan counterattacked. Despite opposition from Barbara Castle, Michael Foot and Benn, he managed to maintain policy in favour of military work for Chile – in turn strengthening the right wing in the AEUW, who, under the influence of John Boyd, succeeded in overturning the existing boycott policy at its September executive. Back in East Kilbride the Rolls Royce shop stewards resisted – refusing work on the engines apart from eventually, in early 1975, putting them back into their crates and dumping them, loosely assembled and without protection, in the yard. Now, however, they were without wider backing from their union and from this point it was the TGWU that carried forward the campaign of active resistance.

The TGWU had campaigned for solidarity from the beginning. Within four days of the coup, on 17 September 1973, the TGWU was lobbying US unions for solidarity; from December 1973 the union imposed a unilateral boycott in the docks; in June 1974, in the midst of the Labour Party battle, it extended the boycott to every aspect of military work for Chile; and in July called on the Labour government to make any settlement of Chilean debt dependent on an end to the Junta's reign of terror. When during the August holiday break in 1975 four of the engines were spirited away out of the yard, Alex Kitson warned that any haulage firm caught handling them would suffer retaliatory action by the TGWU. The four remaining engines continued to rust in the yard till August 1978. At this point the Sheriff Court in Hamilton handed down a judgement that the detention of the engines was illegal. Anyone resisting their movement would face imprisonment. Once more a night-time operation saw the remaining (but now unusable) engines vanish – despite extra vigilance at the docks.

The action by workers in East Kilbride was important in itself. It grounded a significant element of the Junta's offensive weaponry. But it also spurred solidarity action by trade unionists elsewhere. Workers at the Anderson Mavor plant, also in East Kilbride, refused to work on mining equipment destined for Chile. Trade unionists at Weirs boycotted work on pumping equipment. At Rosyth on the East Coast TGWU members did so for Chilean submarines. Probably most notably, on 13 May 1974, workers walked off a Chilean submarine at Yarrow's shipyard in Glasgow (Ann Jones, *No Truck*, p.149).

Again many of those involved, like George Kerr in Renfrew, had already been active in providing help for refugees. The walk-off involved painters, engineers and electricians. One of the painters was Bobby Starrett who as a cartoonist regularly contributed to the TGWU's *Record* in the 1970s. He remembers the painters as the most militant trade in the yard and that many were communists including the yard convener Eddie Kelly. He also remembers the tension on the boat. One of the painters had made friends with a Chilean officer and they talked about politics. 'One day the officer stated that their meetings had to stop at once. The painter said he wasn't worried about the management. The officer stated he was worried about his family back in Chile'. One young apprentice at the time, Tom Morrison, remembers his pride in his workmates and their convener as they walked down the gang plank off the boat (written reminiscence supplied by Tom Morrison and held in the Unite virtual archive, 128 Theobalds Road, London WC1X 8TN, contact Jim Mowat).

Alex Kitson was then the union's deputy general secretary. Prior to the merger with the TGWU in 1972 Alex Kitson had been general secretary of the Scottish Commercial Motormen (SCM). He won that position on a strongly left-wing platform in 1959 and transformed the union into a militant organisation with strongly progressive international links. He became a member of the STUC General Council in 1960 and its president in 1965. He worked with Jim Boyack on the executive of the Labour Party in Scotland to raise the issue of devolution – moving the motion on devolution at the 1968 Labour Party conference with support from the Scottish miners. As general secretary of the SCM he was the first British trade union leader to visit Cuba in 1960. He represented the SCM on the executive of the International Transport Workers Federation and in that capacity campaigned for closer relations between the anti-imperialist World Federation of Trade Unions (WFTU) and the US-linked International Confederation of Free Trade Unions (ICFTU) to which the British TUC was affiliated.

In the 1960s the SCM worked closely with the TGWU in campaigning for better conditions for commercial drivers in Scotland and seeking to secure 100 per cent trade union membership. In this work Kitson developed a close friendship with Jack Jones – both of them champions of the developing shop stewards movement.

After the merger with the TGWU in 1972 Alex Kitson represented the TGWU on the executive of the Labour Party for the following decade and took responsibility for the union's international work. In that capacity he was chair of Anti-Apartheid through the 1970s and 1980s. He played a leading role developing solidarity with Chile, having visited that country, along with Judith Hart MP and Tom Driberg MP just two weeks before the military coup. In the later 1970s and 1980s Kitson continued as a key figure in the campaign for a Scottish Parliament, both before and after the 1978 referendum. He also supported the Left in the mid-1970s in opposing the Labour government's imposition of wage controls as part of the social contract (interviews by John Foster with Irene Kitson and Yvonne Strachan, 2020, Unite Oral History Archive).

7

Ireland: The Difficult Battle for Class Unity

Belfast

In the 1960s and 1970s the giant cranes of the Harland and Wolff shipyard dominated Belfast's skyline. Alongside the shipyard, facing on to Belfast Lough, lay the neat rows of two-up-two-down houses of Protestant East Belfast, accommodation for many of the shipyard's workers. This housing stretched through Cregagh to the Ormeau Road and south Belfast where bigger houses accommodated skilled and professional workers. Towards the centre of Belfast there was a small enclave of Catholic housing in Short Strand and then a larger area of Catholic housing in the Markets. Some of those living there also worked in the yards, mainly as labourers. Across from Belfast's city centre lay West Belfast. This was framed by the line of hills, topped by Divis mountain, that had originally provided the water-power for Belfast's linen mills. Still in the 1960s the mills provided employment for several thousand low-paid female workers. Housing here was some of the worst in Belfast. The area was sharply divided between Protestant households in the Shankill Road and the streets to the north and Catholic houses in the Falls Road and streets to the south. The two roads lay only a few hundred yards apart. There was little contact.

This pattern of housing, reinforced by segregation in education and, very largely, in employment, had been inherited from the nineteenth century and largely framed people's identities. There had been moments when this was challenged, as in 1907 when Catholic and Protestant labourers united for a period against the port employers in the dock strike led by James Larkin. It had been challenged even more decisively during and immediately after the First World War. At this point full employment had for the first time given workers significant power. The end of the war, in January 1919, saw a General Strike as workers demanded a drastic reduction in hours to prevent the return of mass unemployment. The strike was led by Belfast Trades Council and the local committee of the Confederation of Shipbuilding and Engineering Unions. As on Clydeside, the driving force came from the shop stewards in the shipyards and engineering works who effectively ran the city for the best part of four weeks. Representing unskilled workers was Larkin's Irish Transport and General Workers whose Belfast organiser between 1910 and 1914 had been James Connolly. Tom Mann's Workers Union also had a strong presence led by one of Connolly's pupils, Sam Kyle, who became the TGWU's Irish regional secretary from 1931 to 1949 after the Workers Union merger in 1929.

The strike terrified the city's big employers. They conceded a limited reduction in hours – and then made their own preparations. Before the war their political leader, Sir Edward Carson, had created an armed Protestant militia, the Ulster Volunteer Force (UVF), to oppose the plans for Irish Home Rule. It was now revived under the misleading title of the Ulster Democratic Labour Association (UDLA). When mass unemployment returned in 1920 this armed militia enforced mass expulsions from the city's yards and engineering works. Of the 7,000 forced, out two thirds were Catholics and the other third 'socialists', mainly shop stewards, who opposed the expulsions. The expulsions were followed by the burning of Catholic homes and a local pogrom in which hundreds were killed. Later that year, in November 1920, the British government gave the UDLA official status as a regiment, the B Specials. It became a key part of the coercive power of the new Protestant state being established in the North.

This state was based on systematic discrimination. It was so in order to maintain and develop a populist base among Protestant workers and to reinforce religion as the key dividing element within the working class. Protestants got preference in employment and in access to public sector housing – allocated through a local government system entirely gerrymandered to sustain Unionist dominance and with property and residence qualifications maintained for voting.

This was the background to the civil rights movement of the 1960s and early 1970s in which the Amalgamated TGWU (ATGWU) (as it was known in Ireland), and individual ATGWU members in particular, played an important role. The aims of that movement were limited. It was to remove this systematic discrimination and to end the coercive powers of the Unionist Stormont government as exercised through emergency legislation and the B Specials. It was not about Irish unity – nor about socialism. It was, however, designed to remove Unionism's ability to maintain its reactionary political base by dividing working people and thereby weakening the ability of the working-class movement as a whole to strive for wider aims. As a campaign it involved considerable personal courage among those involved and, in the immediate instance, secured only limited success. But it was by no means foolhardy and was founded on the knowledge that the recent past had seen significant periods of cross-community working-class mobilisation.

The basis for this had been laid during the Second World War when, as in 1914–1918, Belfast became a major centre for war production. The

Shorts aircraft company was moved across to Belfast from England at the onset of war on a site directly adjacent to Harland and Wolff. By 1943 the two firms were combined in one company, Harland and Shorts, largely under British government ownership and control, with a joint workforce of 40,000. Between them they contributed a significant part of Britain's war production: 150 warships, 123 merchant ships, 1,200 bombers and over 100 anti-submarine flying boats. In the west of the city the engineering firm James Mackie and Sons produced up to 75 million shells, employing 7,000. A dozen other smaller engineering works employed a further 20,000. The region's linen industry was reorganised to manufacture the fabric for aircraft frames and parachutes and employed 50,000, mainly women. Most of these workers were unionised. Of the trade unions the biggest was the TGWU, strongly placed in transport, retail, chemicals and among non-skilled workers in most sectors of manufacturing. The Irish TGWU (ITGWU) retained a presence in the docks and in the textile industry.[1]

While at the end of the war unionist parties, mainly the Ulster Unionist Party (UUP), maintained their general dominance, the 1945 election for the Stormont Parliament saw the emergence of strong support for a variety of parties representing working-class interests. The Ulster Unionists secured 180,000 votes. The Northern Ireland Labour Party and a variety of other Labour Parties, mainly unionist with a small u, together secured 108,000. The Communist Party gained 12,000 concentrated in Belfast. Nationalists, including Socialist Republicans, gained 37,000. In Belfast itself parties opposed to the Unionists and aligned in one way or other to the labour movement had a significant majority.

Raising Civil Rights and Working-class Unity in Conditions of Sharp Industrial Decline

Over the following two decades employment in Belfast's existing industries shrank – first linen in the fifties followed by shipbuilding and aircraft production and their many supply companies in the early sixties. As in Britain new multinational companies came in – chemicals, synthetics, electronics, consumer products – but usually in locations outside Belfast itself. By 1960 unemployment across the North, at 6.7 per cent, was double that in Britain's most depressed regions, Scotland and Merseyside.

---

1 A Finlay, 'Trade Unionism and Sectarianism among Derry Shirt Workers 1920–1968', PhD thesis (UCL, 1989) found relatively little indication that sectarianism governed the relations between the two major unions, the ITGWU and the National Union of Tailor and Garment Workers (which later merged with the ATGWU). Both unions were relatively militant and members switched between one and the other mainly on the basis of personal loyalties to particular leaders.

By 1963 this had worsened to 7.9 per cent.[2] The Unionist government, under the arrantly sectarian Lord Brookeborough, sought British government money to support the North's unionist employers but resisted plans for more comprehensive modernisation. Brookeborough also rebuffed discussions with the Northern Ireland Committee of the Irish Congress of Trade Unions on the grounds that it was a 'foreign' body. A re-united Irish Congress had finally come into being in 1959–1960 – after three decades of separation – largely through the initiative of the ATGWU under regional secretary Norman Kennedy and of the Irish Transport and General Union, the dominant union in the south.[3] The refusal of the Stormont government to act on unemployment saw mass demonstrations and strikes by the Shorts and Harland workers through the spring of 1961 – with the May Day march of 1961 the biggest since 1919.[4] Trade union organised demonstrations continued into 1962 as the situation worsened and as Brookeborough's Stormont government failed to develop any effective intervention. The Northern Ireland Labour Party made further progress that year in the local elections. The All-Ireland Delegate Conference of ATGWU at Derry in August 1962 unanimously condemned, in a motion from Belfast branches, the Stormont government for continuing to rely on private enterprise and called for a campaign 'to secure acceptance and support for public enterprise' and that a 'combination of industrial and political activity by the trade union movement be organised'. Conference also unanimously passed a resolution condemning the refusal of the Stormont government to recognise the Northern Ireland Committee (NIC) of the Irish Congress of Trade Unions (ICTU).[5]

It was in this context that the NIC of the ICTU launched the first bid to overcome the sectarian divide based on the institutions of the Stormont state. In 1962 and 1963 the NIC conference adopted policy to campaign for civil rights for all, for the non-discriminatory allocation of housing, the ending of discrimination in employment, the repeal of the special powers act and a fully democratic system of representation – without prejudice to the existing state boundaries.[6] In 1964 the NIC ICTU joined with the Northern Ireland (NI) Labour Party to lobby for these policies.[7] In the

---

2 P. Bew, P. Gibbon and H. Patterson, *The State in Northern Ireland* (Manchester University Press, 1979), p.136.

3 T. Cradden, 'The Trade Union Movement in Northern Ireland', in D. Nevin (ed.), *Trade Union Century* (Dublin, 1994), pp.66–84; Charles McCarthy, *Trade Unions in Ireland* (Dublin, 1977).

4 Bew et al., *The State in Northern Ireland*, p.145.

5 ATGWU Records, Unite Offices, 26 Antrim Road, Belfast BT15 2AA.

6 M. McInerney, *Trade Unions Bid for Peace in the North*, articles reprinted from the *Irish Times*, 1970.

7 Cradden, 'Trade Union Movement in Northern Ireland'; Emmett O'Connor, *A Labour History of Ireland 1824–2000* (UCD Press, 2011), pp.275–276, p.281.

ensuing Stormont elections the NI Labour Party won four of the Belfast seats and did so in 'Protestant' working-class constituencies.

This was in the context of widespread anger at Stormont's failure to arrest industrial decline. At this stage the main organisation which expressed this anger was Belfast and District Trades Council. Its delegates represented trade union branches across the wider Belfast area. Average attendance ranged around 70 and exceeded 100 at annual general meetings. It was this body, in the years when the NIC was not recognised by Stormont, which had acted as the trade union movement's main interface with the Stormont government. Its full-time secretary was Betty Sinclair, a TGWU member (previously Tailor and Garment Workers). Its chair was Joe Cooper, also TGWU and later on the union's full-time Irish regional officer for commercial transport.

Together they represented the diversity of Belfast's working class and at the same time the bonds of the trade union and class understanding that united it. Betty Sinclair came from a Protestant background. She had previously been a trade union activist in the Belfast linen mills and was a communist. Joe Cooper was a Catholic.[8] His father had been a dockside carter who worked with Jim Larkin in the 1907 dockers strike and was a pioneer of the carters' union. Joe himself became a carter, joined the TGWU and soon became an organiser. He was a friend of both Frank Cousins and Jack Jones, eventually becoming transport organiser for Ireland and was a committed supporter of the Northern Ireland Civil Rights Association (NICRA). Between them Sinclair and Cooper maintained the unity of an otherwise fractious trades council in a period when the challenges were not just those of sectarianism but, underlying this division, an experience of de-industrialisation on a scale only seen later across the Irish sea in Britain in the 1980s. This decline, a loss of industrial jobs that most affected the previously protected Protestant workforce, is registered in the changing composition of the trades council itself. In the 1950s there were 45 industrial branches affiliated and six public sector. By 1980 there were only ten industrial and 30 public sector.[9] It was this industrial decline, as the TWGU's Ireland educational organiser Sean Morrisey wrote in 1978, that fuelled sectarian attitudes – but which also made the focus on immediate class issues the necessary starting point for any progressive change.[10]

It was the Belfast Trades Council that called the first conference to mobilise wider support for the call for civil rights, in the context of

8 Eugene McGlone, later TGWU Irish regional organiser, interview by John Foster, September 2020, Unite Oral History Archive; Kevin Cooper, son of Joe Cooper, interview by John Foster, September 2020, Unite Oral History Archive.

9 Eugene McGlone, 'The Belfast Trades Council: Political Hegemony and Civil Rights', Master's thesis (University of Ulster, 1986).

10 M. Morrisey and S. Morrisey, 'Northern Ireland: Why the Trade Unions Are Central', *Marxism Today*, November 1979.

campaigning on issues of employment and industrial development. The 1964 elections had seen Brookeborough replaced as Unionist leader by Terence O'Neill who adopted a less hostile attitude to the Catholic population, spoke out against sectarian prejudice and recognised the NIC of ICTU. However, he made no move to dismantle any element of the institutional structure that sustained sectarian discrimination. The conference was designed to mobilise opinion, particularly among the wider Protestant population, for action on this front – linking it to demands for wider unity around issues of industrial decline and unemployment. The conference was held in May 1965 in the headquarters of the TGWU in Belfast and attended by a range of trade union leaders, mainly in personal capacity, including members of the ATGWU, Sheet Metal Workers, Engineers, printers and the scientific staff union Draughtmens and Allied Technicians Association (DATA) (whose regional officer was then Ken Gill). The conference called for detailed discussions in the trade union movement and for further campaigning initiatives. These came in January 1967 with the formal establishment of NICRA at a conference in the International Hotel attended by the officers of the trades council, representatives of both the Northern Ireland Labour Party and the Young Unionists, of tenants associations, of the republican Wolfe Tone societies and a range of trade unions. The following year, 1968, the trades council secretary, Betty Sinclair, was elected as chair.[11]

By then strains were developing within the UUP. Ministers on its right-wing loyalist wing, such as William Craig, were using their powers to further restrict civil liberties and banned the Republican clubs. There was also increasing tacit collusion with the revival of loyalist militias involving Reverend Ian Paisley. NICRA initially concentrated on discrimination in housing, occupying a limited number of houses unfairly allocated by gerrymandered councils and organising wider protest marches. In August 1968 a peaceful march to Dungannon was attacked by Paisley loyalists. In October a protest march in Derry was attacked by the Royal Ulster Constabulary (RUC) and B Specials – who then went on an indiscriminate rampage in the Catholic Bogside area of Derry. By autumn 1968 the British prime minister Wilson was calling on O'Neill to initiate reforms.

Still at this point probably most workers from a Protestant background did not dissent from the initiatives on civil rights – and a majority of those involved in NICRA themselves came from that background. The TGWU moved carefully. In face of much bolder demands from some British regions at the union's biennial conference in 1967, the meeting decided to take no formal position. 'It was recognised that none of the motions had

11 Madge Davidson, *We Shall Overcome: History of the Struggle for Civil Rights in Northern Ireland 1968–1978* (republished Belfast and District Trades Council, 2019); Lynda Walker (ed.), *Madge Davidson: Recollections* (Shanway Press, 2011).

been submitted in Region 11 there being a tacit understanding that having regard to the make-up of the membership which includes all shapes of political opinion in Ireland it was realistic to pursue a policy which would raise members earnings and standards of living rather than being preoccupied with an objective on which the membership was divided'.[12]

Change, it indicated, had to come from within the North itself and from within the established organisations of the trade union and labour movement. This assessment may sound unduly cautious but it would seem to have been vindicated by subsequent developments. In 1968–1969 a minority caucus of students from Queens University sought to take over NICRA in the name of 'Peoples Democracy' and embarked on confrontationalist tactics against the RUC. Although by later 1969 Betty Sinclair and the Belfast Trades Council had managed to resecure trade union leadership within NICRA, the damage had been done. Many of NICRA's Protestant supporters in workplaces had withdrawn. Similarly in 1970 the Irish Republican Army, previously endorsing the class unity policies of NICRA and adopting a purely defensive role in Catholic/republican areas, split. In face of the more aggressive stance of the British army from 1970 and heightened activity by Protestant paramilitaries, its Provisional wing adopted an active military campaign against Stormont and the British Army.[13]

The O'Neill government collapsed under these tensions in 1969. After a further Stormont election Chichester-Clark took over as prime minister but ultimately proved unable to handle the level of dissent from the party's right wing. In June 1969 the RUC again went on the rampage in Derry after a further civil rights protest. This resulted in the death of one man, a Catholic, the first of many deaths during the troubles. In August 1969 further serious rioting occurred in both Derry and Belfast, involving both the RUC and B Specials, causing Wilson to send in British troops. Along with other pressures, lobbying by NIC of ICTU, led by the ATGWU regional secretary Norman Kennedy, then resulted in a British government review of policing under General Sir John Hunt. His report called for the disbanding of the B Specials, a reform of the police, a central body to oversee public sector housing, an agency to investigate discrimination in employment and a reform of voting. Chichester-Clark incorporated these in Stormont government policy in the autumn of 1969.[14] Formally at least a number of the key demands of the civil rights movement had been achieved.

However, the Tory election victory in June 1970 saw a significant, if unspoken, reversal of policy. British troops started to take a tougher line in

12 MRC MSS 126/TG/1887/22, Record of Decisions, July 1963, p.3.

13 NICRA's *We Shall Overcome*, as written in 1978 by its then Secretary Madge Davidson, offers significant evidence of funding by right-wing Fianna Fail ministers for those who formed the Provisional IRA. This is further evidenced by B. Hanley and S. Millar, *The Lost Revolution* (Penguin Ireland, 2009), pp.136–144.

14 McInerney, *Trade Unions Bid for Peace.*

policing. Five Catholics were killed in West Belfast in July 1970. In March 1971 the hardliner Brian Faulkner replaced Chichester-Clark and in August 1971 imposed internment without trial – including some leaders of the NICRA and ATGWU officer Sean Morrisey.[15] In January 1972 the British army shot dead 13 unarmed civilians at a peaceful NICRA rally in Derry. Three ATGWU members in the front ranks were among those killed: Patrick Docherty, Michael McDaid and Jim Wray. Speaking at the annual Congress of the ICTU that summer as Irish regional secretary of the ATGWU, Norman Kennedy stressed the links between sectarian division and the failure of the movement to secure full employment – and the links between de-industrialisation and job loss and sectarian hostility: 'full employment in Northern Ireland would mean the end of one of the main causes of feelings of inequality, namely the lack of equality in the right to a job'.[16]

In March 1972 Direct Rule was imposed and Stormont abolished. Over the following years many workplaces were bombed, whole areas of housing destroyed and 3,600 people killed.[17]

'They Mingled Together With Consciousness of the Difference Between Them'[18]

As sectarian violence intensified after the abolition of Stormont in 1972, Norman Kennedy told the July meeting of ATGWU's Regional Committee:

> the one beacon of hope has been the successful effort by the trade union movement to maintain the unity of workers, Catholic and Protestant, on the shop floor. Despite the terrors and strains that the conflict on the streets, the bombings and shootings, have created, trade union officials, shop stewards and other trade union activists have succeeded in keeping the strife between the two communities out of the factories and offices. It has been a notable achievement in a divided community torn apart by bitterness, hatred and sectarianism. It is an achievement of which we in the trade union movement are intensely proud.[19]

---

15 'Belfast Trade Unionist Dedicated to Working-Class Unity', *The Irish Times*, 13 February 2016. Sean Morrisey had also been imprisoned in the 1940s for IRA membership.

16 Matt Merrigan, *Eagle or Cuckoo: The Story of the ATGWU in Ireland* (Matmer Publications, 1989), pp.238–239.

17 Brian Campfield (TGWU 11/38 branch; president ICTU 2016–2017), 'Trade Unions and Peace in Northern Ireland', unpublished paper (UniGlobal, 2019).

18 John Darby, *Conflict in Northern Ireland: The Development of a Polarised Community* (Gill and Macmillan, 1976), p.73.

19 ATGWU regional minutes, 1 July 1972, ATGWU office, Antrim Road, Belfast.

There is therefore both a striking similarity, and a striking difference, to what was happening across the sea in Britain. At precisely the same time, in July–August 1972, the working-class movement in Britain forced a massive government retreat and demonstrated a level of unity and solidarity in action not seen since the 1926 General Strike. In Britain a mobilised working class had been able to change the balance of class power. Nothing like this happened in Ireland. But there was also a common factor. If there was any success in the North, a major one in the circumstances, it was the understanding that an appeal to class unity, practically related to immediate economic challenges, was the only way to exclude open sectarian strife from the workplace.

Those who led this continuing fight for class unity seem have been somewhat different in terms of age and experience from those who led the wages struggle in Britain. They tended to be older, going back to the generation of trade union activists who developed during the full employment of the Second World War. At that point the level of workplace militancy, in terms of strike action, was three times that in Britain.[20] For the ATGWU this relatively high level of disputes appears to have continued on until 1971. For the four years 1968 to 1971 the number of disputes officially recognised by the TGWU was, in proportion to population, running around three times the number in Scotland and the West Midlands – and, despite the troubles, membership continued to rise into the early months of 1971 though declined thereafter.[21] It was also an older generation of branch officers who are remembered as dominating the meetings of Belfast Trades Council rather than the relatively new and young generation of shop stewards as on the Clyde, Mersey and in London.[22]

In Britain it was the political courage of this younger generation that provided a leadership that was able to unite and mobilise a much wider movement among working people from many diverse backgrounds. In Ireland the achievement of this older generation was more defensive but critical nonetheless. It was what they managed to stop. In contrast to what happened in 1920–1922, and to a lesser degree in 1934–1935, there were no large-scale workplace expulsions on sectarian lines. This was no accident. It was the result of constant vigilance, personal courage and, most critically, the ability to argue for the maintenance of unity on class lines.

One TGWU steward, a member of the 11/38 bakers branch and from a Catholic background, remembers intervening in a large bakery in West Belfast, predominantly Catholic. It was after one of the rampages by B

20 Cradden, 'Trade Union Movement in Northern Ireland'.

21 TGWU General Executive Committee minutes, Disputes for 1968, 1969, 1970 and 1971. minutes of the ATGWU Quarterly, January, April and July 1971, TGWU records Antrim Road office, Belfast.

22 This is the assessment of Eugene McGlone, interview by John Foster, September 2020, Unite Oral History Archive.

Figure 5: Joe Cooper, outgoing chair of Belfast Trades Council,
hands over the banner to Liam McBrinn, also a TGWU officer, in
Transport House, Belfast
(from Kevin Cooper)

Specials in which scores of houses had been burnt out and many injured.
The following day he spotted the one Protestant worker, a storeman,
packing up his belongings to leave the bakery. He told him not to leave,
and discovered the source of threats was a Catholic worker whose family
has lost their home. He discussed this with him and then called a meeting
and stressed the need to maintain their own unity as workers. No worker
left the bakery. Some years later he was working in the Ormeau bakery in
the strongly Protestant South Belfast. He had eventually, on the basis of his
effective actions as a shop steward, been elected convener. In this capacity
he raised with his fellow workers the continuing presence throughout the
workplace of loyalist regalia, flags and bunting, months after the 12 July
parades, as intimidating to non-Protestants. He won agreement to raise it
with the management who reluctantly agreed to its removal. A couple of
weeks later, but outside the workplace, he was shot and seriously wounded
by loyalist gunmen.[23]

His bakers branch of the ATGWU, a big one with around 2,000
members, was one of the most consistently left-wing branches in the
region. In the period 1971–1974 it submitted motions calling for support

23 Pearse McKenna, interview by John Foster, September 2020, Unite Oral History
Archive; 'Trade Union Official Shot by Ulster Extremists', *Reuters*, 5 October 1991.

for the LCDTU and full opposition to the Industrial Relations Bill in January 1971. In January 1973 it was criticising the union for not sufficiently actively combatting sectarianism and successfully called for a special branch conference on the subject, and in April asked for continued detailed anti-sectarian work in branches.[24]

For the trade union movement as a whole the first major test came in August 1969. The RUC and B Specials had launched an assault on Catholic West Belfast resulting in a significant number of casualties. There were expectations of further violence and retaliation. On 14 August there were rumours that Catholics would, as had happened in a previous generation, be expelled from Belfast's biggest employer, the predominantly Protestant Harland and Wolff shipyard. Shop stewards, Catholic and Protestant, gathered that afternoon and called a mass meeting for the next day. They issued the following statement to be put to the meeting:

This mass meeting of shipyard workers calls on the people of Northern Ireland for the immediate restoration of peace throughout the country. We recognise that the continuation of the present disorder can only end in economic disaster [...] We recommend to this mass meeting that there should be a token stoppage at 3.30 today as an expression of our concern and determination to maintain peace and good will in the yard and throughout the province.[25]

That night there was indeed a further RUC assault on West Belfast and the erection of barricades to protect Catholic neighbourhoods. The following afternoon, despite threats to individual stewards, the mass meeting took place and the resolution passed unanimously. Subsequently stewards from the yard were allowed through the barricades into West Belfast to call on Catholic workers to return to work – and in Protestant East Belfast they held meetings which successfully countered attempts by right-wing paramilitaries to organise attacks.

The ability of the joint stewards committee to take these initiatives was based on the effectiveness of their past stand in defending jobs, wages and conditions and the degree to which the committee embraced all unions within the yards, from technical staff to labourers. The success of the stewards at Harland and Wolff on 15 August also empowered other stewards – at Shorts, at International Computers and at Grundig in Lisburn – to take similar action. Many of these stewards had graduated

24 ATGWU Quarterly minutes 4 January 1971, 8 January 1973 and 3 April 1973, Unite Offices, 26 Antrim Road, Belfast BT15 2AA.
25 McInerny, *Trade Unions Bid for Peace*, p.8.

from the political school of Belfast Trades Council and most were on the Left. But. most important of all, working-class unity was not, for them, an abstract concept. In the streets of Belfast they could see the consequences of its opposite.

The autumn of 1969 saw the successful lobbying of the Wilson government by the NIC of ICTU, and more informally by Jack Jones and the TGWU in London, which resulted in the Hunt Report and commitment by the Stormont government to its implementation.[26] However, this advance was, as we saw, short-lived. Within a few months the Unionist right wing had taken over at Stormont and the return of a Conservative government in Westminster saw a significant shift to harder line policies by both Stormont and the British military, with the introduction of internment leading to an extension of the paramilitary defence of Catholic communities. Bloody Sunday and the dissolution of Stormont, the symbol of Protestant ascendancy, then saw the right wing of the Unionist Party move into active alliance with Protestant paramilitaries. Their objective was to overthrow the Heath government's attempt to create a power-sharing executive. The Ulster Workers Council's 'strike' of May 1974, taking place just after Labour had replaced the Tories in Westminster, marked the climax of this intervention.

Its form reveals an awareness in the ranks of the intransigent Unionists of the degree to which they had not so far broken trade union unity. The 'Workers Council' was in fact a federation of paramilitaries operating under aegis of UUP godfathers. Its description as a 'workers' council' was required in order to give it popular legitimacy. Similarly, its action to paralyse NI economically was called 'a strike', yet in no major workplace did the paramilitaries win the vote for a strike. Workers condemned it. In the biggest – Harland and Wolff – in a previous generation a bastion of Unionism, the vote was decisive. The paramilitaries then burnt leading shop stewards' cars in the carpark. The lockout was based on intimidation.

One trade union officer who worked to maintain this workplace unity, the president of the NI Confed for most of the following decade, noted that enforcement depended on two things. One was the blocking of all motorways and major roads with barricades which, because of their number, were usually defended by only handfuls of paramilitaries. The other was the failure of the local authorities to make any attempt to clear the barricades – despite the presence of thousands of British troops and an armed police force. Mervyn Rees, recently arrived with a couple of junior ministers, appears to have been told by local administrators that it was too dangerous to do so. Yet in a significant number of workplaces

---

26 Baron Hunt, "Report of The Advisory Committee on Police in Northern Ireland", October 1969, Belfast: Her Majesty's Stationery Office.

trade unionists took action themselves to insist that the management kept workplaces open.[27]

A 'march back to work' two weeks into the lockout was initiated by stewards in Harland and Wolff led by their convener Andy Holmes. It won the wider backing of all unions. The regional leadership of the ATGWU gave full support and Len Murray, the general secretary of the TUC, was brought over to lead it. Norman Kennedy was among the marchers. His report to the subsequent June executive condemned the lockout as a 'political stoppage' and noted 'the widespread intimidation of those desiring to march and indeed of those reporting or wishing to report for work'.[28] Despite the presence of Len Murray, the march was given only token military protection in face of a massive paramilitary mobilisation. Many of those trying to get to the assembly point were stopped, including John Freeman, subsequent ATGWU regional secretary.[29] The march itself was surrounded by stone-throwing paramilitaries. One participant described the young squaddies sent to give protection as turning to flee before being ordered back into place by officers. It was, commented another participant, the nearest he had come to seeing fascism at first hand.[30] Eventually around 200 marched and, and despite injuries, managed to reach the gates of Harland and Wolff. A smaller contingent, led by ATGWU officer Ernie McBride, marched up the Castlereagh Road through Protestant Cregagh to International Computers where McBride was senior steward.[31] The following day, *The Times* headline described it as 'Almost Total Failure'.[32] Two days later Wilson reported to Cabinet from a Chequers meeting with the officers of the power-sharing executive, Faulkner, Fitt and Napier, that the lockout was 'essentially an attempt by extremists to establish an unacceptable form of neo-fascist government'.[33] The executive fell a week later.

The June minute of the ATGWU June regional committee was somewhat different in tone: 'the trade union movement was built up by steadfastness to principle in season and out of season, and we should continue to propound those principles and continue our efforts to

27 Joe Bowers, DATA/TASS officer, regional Confed president 1980s, interview by John Foster, August 2020, Unite Oral History Archive.

28 Mick O'Reilly, *A Life on the Left* (Lilliput, 2019), p.68; O'Reilly, interview by John Foster, October 2020, Unite Oral History Archive.

29 Mick O'Reilly, interview by John Foster, 2020.

30 Joe Bowers, interview by John Foster, August 2020, Unite Oral History Archive.

31 Paul Arthur, *Government and Politics of Northern Ireland* (Longman, 1980) cites Robert Fisk, *Point of No Return* (Deutsch, 1975), p.230, that British army commanders determined policy independently of Rees and Orme with indications of partiality towards the lockout organisers.

32 Robert Fisk in *The Times*, 22 May 1974.

33 TNA CAB 129/177/20, Hunt to Cabinet 24 May 1974.

reconstruct a society where social justice, peace, equality of opportunity and prosperity are our objective'. The 200 who marched – Protestant and Catholic – were, like TGWU officer Joe Cooper, mainly from that generation who had carried forward the initiatives of Belfast Trades Council and of NICRA over the previous two decades.

When workplaces reassembled early in June trade union stewards reassumed their functions without question. Although the paramilitaries may, in the course of the lockout, have succeeded in mobilising Protestant communities, they failed in their subsequent efforts to replace existing trade union structures in workplaces and establish a sectarian 'Ulster' trade union structure. This was an achievement – albeit a negative one – of great importance for the future of all those living in the North.[34]

Ireland: Challenging Sexual Inequalities
How the ATGWU Led the Way

Alex Klemm

In 1970 the ICTU submission to the Commission on the Status of Women noted that women's hourly earnings were 55 per cent those of men. In 1976 a study published in the Economic and Social Review used a 1972 dataset constructed from the Department of Labour's redundancy payments database, supplemented with survey data, and found that weekly earnings for males were 73 per cent higher than for females. The differential was not explained by differences in characteristics.[35]

Ireland's accession to the EEC in 1973 was followed by the 1974 Anti-Discrimination (Pay) Act. This Act, which was introduced to comply with Ireland's obligations under EC legislation and also in response to pressure from women's groups, trade unions and the Commission on the Status of Women, was due to come into force on 31 December 1975. The Act introduced into all contracts of employment an equality clause, entitling women to equal pay with men (or vice versa) where they were employed on 'like work'.

---

34 This is the assessment of Mick O'Reilly, Ernie McBride and Eugene McGlone, interview by John Foster, October 2020, Unite Oral History Archive.
35 B. Walsh and B. Whelan, 'A Micro-Economic Study of Earnings in Ireland', *The Economic and Social Review*, 1976, vol.7. no.2, pp.199–217, cited in A. Doris, 'Ireland's Gender Wage Gap, Past and Present', *The Economic and Social Review*. 2019, vol.50, no.4, pp.667–681.

The Inequality Context

In the 1960s and early 1970s approximately one third of the Irish workforce was female, but it was clustered in a narrow range of occupations, tended to be younger and less experienced than men, and around four in five working women were single.[36] This was due not only to social attitudes but also to the marriage bar which obtained in the civil service, in sectors such as banking and in large private sector employers such as Jacobs.

There were four general workers' unions in Ireland: the Irish Transport and General Workers' Union (ITGWU), with approximately 150,000 members in the 1960s;[37] the Workers' Union of Ireland with around 50,000,[38] the Irish Women Workers' Union, with approximately 3,000 members,[39] and the Amalgamated Transport and General Workers' Union, reported as having 17,000 members in the Republic in 1969[40] rising to 30,000 in 1975.[41]

Pay differentials both between women and men (and between men and 'boys' and women and 'girls') were accepted not only by wider society but also by the trade union movement. In the late 1940s the P.J. Carroll's cigarette factory in Dundalk had an overwhelmingly female workforce. ATGWU district secretary Gilbert Lynch and ITGWU leader William O'Brien divided up the workforce, with the ATGWU taking the women and the ITGWU the men: the rationale was each union would derive equal benefit from the arrangement, since while the ATGWU gained more members the women in question earned less and thus paid less in dues.[42] Unions regularly negotiated pay deals incorporating different pay scales and percentage increases for women and men.

Both the Transport and General Workers' Union and its Irish section, the Amalgamated Transport and General Workers' Union, were forced to confront the issue of pay discrimination not only on behalf of women members but internally. In October 1970, the *Irish Times* reported that the union itself throughout Britain and Ireland was facing the threat of strike action over pay differentials:

36 Mary Daly, *Women and Work in Ireland* (Dublin, 1997) as cited in M. Ayres, 'Equal pay for women: words not deeds?', *Saothar* (journal of the Irish Labour History Society), 2011, vol.36, pp.89–96.

37 *Dáil Éireann debate*, 5 March 1969, vol. 238, no.15.

38 Arthur Marsh and John B. Smethurst, *Historical Directory of Trade Unions*, vol.5 (Routledge, 2006), pp.497–499.

39 M. Ayres, 'Equal pay for women: words not deeds?', *Saothar*, vol.36, pp.89–96.

40 *Irish Times*, 27 November 1969 (membership in the Republic).

41 *Irish Times*, 22 March 1975.

42 Conversation between Alex Klemm and former ATGWU regional secretary Mick O'Reilly, 13 May 2021.

The Amalgamated Transport and General Workers' Union is faced with an embarrassing dispute. About 130 girls employed in its offices in Ireland, Scotland and Yorkshire have threatened to stage a series of one-day strikes over a pay claim. An official of the union admitted reluctantly yesterday that clerks, typists, ledger clerks and cashiers 'are contemplating action to secure satisfaction in their claim'. The union calls them 'staff' to distinguish them from its officials. The girls have been offered a 7.5 percent increase on their present basic pay of £17.5s a week. Although they were dissatisfied with the offer it has been put into their pay packets. They are claiming an increase of £5 per week. All the girls employed by the union, a total of 500, are involved in the claim. The union's officials, the men who administer it and lead its negotiations, are sympathetic to the claim.[...] Only the girls in Ireland, Scotland and Yorkshire are threatening action.[43]

Both before and after the introduction of equal pay legislation, the trade union response to pay discrimination was anaemic. In 1970, around 100,000 women were members of trade unions including around 49,000 in the Irish Transport and General Workers' Union and 7,000 in the smaller Amalgamated Transport and General Workers' Union.

Historian Margaret Ayres has noted:

It might have been expected that Irish trade unions would have campaigned vigorously in favour of equal pay, as a basic human right, for their female members, but this was not the case. Although resolutions were regularly passed in its favour, action to achieve equal pay was notably lacking, especially in the case of private sector unions. Employers, journalists and government ministers were all aware that the unions often paid only lip service to women's rights.[44]

Ayres's criticism was largely focused on the action or inaction of the ITGWU. Under the leadership of Matt Merrigan, district secretary for the Republic of Ireland from 1960 to 1986, the smaller ATGWU pursued an active strategy of centralised and workplace bargaining to secure equal pay for its women members. In 1969 the first of the ATGWU's claims for equal pay was served on the biscuit manufacturers W&R Jacobs Ltd, around 800 of whose 1,500 workers were females.[45]

43 *Irish Times*, 6 October 1970.
44 M. Ayres, 'Equal pay for women: words not deeds?', *Saothar*, vol.36, pp.89–96.
45 *Irish Times*, 27 November 1969.

Jacobs's iconic place in Dublin's industrial history dated back to the 1913 lockout, when management put up a notice prohibiting the wearing of union badges on the premises. Three workers who refused to handle flour from a mill which had locked out its workers were subsequently dismissed, resulting in a prolonged strike and lockout involving 14 per cent of the female workforce and 63 per cent of the male workforce; the dispute, largely involving members of Jim Larkin's Irish Transport and General Workers' Union, lasted from August 1913 until March 1914.[46] Since then, industrial peace was maintained until 1961 when the workforce – now mainly represented by the ATGWU and the Workers' Union of Ireland – went on strike after rejecting an offered increase of £1 a week for men and 13s 6d for women.[47] Unions were seeking an increase of 32/6 for men and 25/3 for women.[48] The dispute was short-lived, with workers accepting a subsequent increase – recommended by unions – of 21/6 and 14/6 respectively for men and women.[49]

Given the high levels of union density in Jacobs, as well as the workforce composition, it was the obvious target for the ATGWU's first equal pay claim in November 1969. The *Irish Times* reported that craftsmen working for Jacobs had secured an increase of £4 10/-, and that the union's claim sought to restore operatives' relativity with craftsmen and give the same increase to men and women; the paper noted that a smaller increase would be expected for girls.[50]

While the claim was not entirely successful, the outcome did represent a significant advance. In January 1970 the Jacobs Joint Negotiating Committee comprising the ATGWU, the Workers' Union of Ireland and the Irish Bakers, Confectioners and Allied Workers' Union recommended acceptance of an offer which would see men receive a phased increase of £4 over two years as against 72s for women over the same period, with smaller increases for boys and girls. Under the agreement, adult females received 90 per cent of the male increase, compared to 80 per cent under the previous agreement.[51] Members were balloted and voted to accept the deal.[52]

Although the gender differential in Jacobs had been substantially narrowed, it had not yet been eliminated.

---

46 P. McCaffrey, 'Jacob's Women Workers during the 1913 Lockout', *Saothar*, 1991, vol.16, pp.118–129.

47 *Irish Times*, 4 December 1961.

48 *Irish Times*, 9 December 1961.

49 *Irish Times*, 13 December 1961.

50 *Irish Times*, 27 November 1969.

51 *Irish Times*, 8 January 1970.

52 *Irish Times*, 13 January 1970.

Centralised Bargaining and National Wage Agreements

In advance of the equal pay legislation promised for 1976, much of the trade union effort (such as it was) to secure equal pay focused on centralised bargaining and national wage agreements. Under the leadership of Matt Merrigan, the ATGWU opposed centralised wage bargaining. In his memoirs, Merrigan summed up the union's position:

> National Wage Agreements (NWAs) were in vogue in the 70s having been forced on a not unwilling ICTU Executive, the majority of public sector and white collar unions and the ITGWU leading the charge under threat of restrictive legislation by the Fianna Fail Government in 1969. The policy of the ATGWU was against centralised bargaining because the norm emerging from such arrangements would be the lowest common denominator, regardless of profitable sectors being in a position to pay more.[53]

Each NWA was preceded by a special conference of the ICTU which gave the Congress executive a negotiating mandate[54]. Notwithstanding his opposition to centralised bargaining and NWAs, Merrigan repeatedly used these special conferences to advance the cause of equal pay while retaining a focus on workplace-level bargaining.

Even before the first of the NWAs in 1970s, when negotiations started for the twelfth national round of wage increases in November 1969, the ATGWU announced that it was seeking the same increases for women as for men. Speaking to the *Irish Times*, Merrigan stated that, on average, women were paid 51 per cent of men's rates and said: 'We feel that the differential between men and women should be narrowed. We believe that it should help reverse the trend of industries being tailored to suit very low women's rates. Our policy should be an instalment in narrowing the differential'.[55]

Where women's work could be seen to be of equal value to that performed by their male colleagues, the ATGWU argued that they should receive equal pay, and where an assessment as equal was not possible 'the differential be only 10 percent *in accordance with an international trend*'.

In 1972 – when the union was reported as representing 25,000 workers in the Republic – the ATGWU rejected a new NWA by a majority of 15 to one. The proposed agreement, negotiated by the Employer-Labour Conference (which represented the government as an employer, state

---

53 Matt Merrigan, *Eggs and Rashers: Irish Socialist Memories*, ed. D.R. O'Connor-Lysaght (Umiskin Press, 2014).
54 S. Cody, J. O'Dowd, and P. Rigney, *The Parliament of Labour: 100 Years of the Dublin Council of Trade Unions* (Dublin Council of Trade Unions, 1986), pp.227–228.
55 *Irish Times*, 27 November 1969.

companies, the main national employer bodies and the ICTU) was set to run for 15 months and provided for a minimum increase of £2.25 per week for men and £2 for women.[56]

In 1973 the ICTU held a special delegate conference to mandate the executive to negotiate a successor agreement, with delegates voting 256 to 123 in favour. Once again the ATGWU was among the unions opposing a new agreement. Reporting on the mood of the conference, the *Irish Times* noted that 'a 1973 national agreement will have to bring more benefit to women workers than its two most recent predecessors. Women delegates were dissatisfied with the rate of progress towards equal pay'.[57]

By 1974, the campaign for equal pay was gaining momentum. National agreements had started to make inroads on the differential. In August 1974, the *Irish Times* reported that the average hourly earnings of around 66,000 women in industry had been increasing more rapidly than those of men. Between 31 December 1970 and 31 December 1973, women's earnings increased by 67 per cent and men's by 54 per cent, yet women's earnings were still only around 58 per cent of men's earnings, with women working shorter hours and doing less shift work.[58]

In 1974, the unions were again preparing for a special delegate conference on a new national agreement, and with regard to the equal pay issue, the *Irish Times* noted that:

> Employers appear worried about the cost of granting equal pay. They are fortunate in that the unions have been inexplicably lackadaisical about obtaining for their women members in the private sector the advances towards it promised under both the 1972 and 1974 national agreements, while the public sector unions have advanced more rapidly that these agreements proposed. The law now requires full implementation by the end of 1975, which is two years earlier than the target date recommended by the Commission on the Status of Women. The Federated Union of Employers has little reason to be hopeful about its plea to the Government on 26 September for a more gradual programme.[59]

In 1974 the first general national equal pay claim was served on the bacon industry, while claims were also served on companies in the sugar confectionary sector.[60]

Notwithstanding sectoral and workplace equal pay claims, the trade union movement's main instrument in the struggle for equal pay remained

56 *Irish Times*, 22 June 1972.
57 *Irish Times*, 28 September 1973.
58 *Irish Times*, 19 August 1974.
59 *Irish Times*, 7 October 1974.
60 *Irish Times*, 19 August 1974.

NWAs, which the ATGWU continued opposing, despite the fact that – as pointed out by the *Irish Times*[61] – TGWU general secretary Jack Jones had been the main architect of a corresponding social contract in Britain. The difference, of course, was that Jones was operating under a Labour government, while the Irish trade union movement in the 1970s was operating under a Conservative Fine Gael–Labour coalition.

Evaluation or Equality?

The equal pay clauses in the 1974 and draft 1975 National Pay Agreements centred on job evaluation as a means of determining whether women were entitled to the same basic equal pay as their main colleagues. In 1975, this approach was rejected by conferences of women members of both the ITGWU and the ATGWU, with the latter holding that the approach would perpetuate and institutionalise discrimination against woman.[62]

A conference of ATGWU women members, held on 21 March 1975, rejected the job evaluation approach as perpetuating and institutionalising discrimination, and also urged the union to vote against the draft 1975 agreement on the basis that the four-phase percentage increases it offered would widen the differentials between male and female pay.[63] A conference of women members of the ITGWU had similarly rejected the evaluation approach.[64]

Instead, the conference called for the 1974 Anti-Discrimination (Pay) Act to be amended to provide for common basic wage criteria for men and women, while also making it clear that it did not intend to rely on legislation to drive pay equality.

The union said it would be instructing its officers to call special branch meetings to decide strategy and timetables for equal pay claims which, if necessary, would be supported by industrial action. The ambitious timetable proposed by the ATGWU envisaged 25 per cent of the differential between male and female basic rates to be paid on 1 July 1975, with a further 25 per cent of the remaining differential to be paid on 1 January 1976, 25 per cent of the remainder on 1 July 1976 and the remaining 25 per cent on 1 January 1977.[65]

Pointing out that the equal pay commissioner had failed to recommend equal pay for confectioners and hairdressers, Matt Merrigan told the conference that the ATGWU was insisting on equalisiation of pay and working conditions over 18 months using its own industrial bargaining and

61 *Irish Times*, 7 October 1974.
62 *Irish Times*, 22 March 1975.
63 *Irish Times*, 22 March 1975.
64 *Irish Times*, 22 March 1975.
65 *Irish Times*, 22 March 1975.

pressure with the support of its male members, rather than the elaborate procedures of national agreements. The *Irish Times* reported that Merrigan went on to say that the time had gone when the union could allow employers to maintain women workers as an exploited sub-stratum of the working class 'with the unthinking status-soaked prejudiced ignorance of some of our male members'.[66]

In a leader comment on the ATGWU women's conference headlined 'The Case for Women', the *Irish Times* led off by reminding readers that 'Mr Merrigan may not be a very representative trade unionist, although he is sincere and dedicated' and surmising that '[t]here may be many in the trade union movement who will not agree with the aggressive equal pay policy which he announced yesterday after a national conference of women members of his union', but went on to state:

'But it must be admitted that over the past 2½ years the equal pay campaign has lacked energy and conviction in so far as it affects women in private enterprise employment. The great majority of them have yet to receive any benefit from it. Worse still, the unions appear to have sought benefit for only a minority of them. Mr Merrigan is justified in his assertion that the equal pay clauses of the 1972 and 1974 agreements "have proved unsatisfactory and frustrating", and in criticising the inclusion of those of the latter in the 1975 agreement'.

The leader concluded by asking 'Are the national employer bodies and the Irish Congress of Trade Unions depending on legislation to resolve equal pay issues?'[67]

Deferral of Equal Pay Legislation
By 1975 it was clear that employer bodies were preparing to wage a campaign against the proposed equal pay legislation – and that the reservations expressed by the ATGWU and the wider trade union movement regarding job evaluation in centralised agreements were more than justified. The Federated Union of Employers' (FUE) strategy was, on the one hand, to press for an inclusion of 'inability-to-pay' clauses in the legislation, similar to those obtaining in NWAs, and to focus on 'job evaluation techniques' to achieve what FUE official John Dunne described as 'an orderly transition' on equal pay. Dunne was addressing an FUE conference which also heard from George Webb, Director of Research for the UK Engineering Employers' Federation. Webb described the purpose of job evaluation as

66 *Irish Times*, 22 March 1975.
67 *Irish Times* (leader), 22 March 1975.

'to produce a graded hierarchy of jobs which reflect the social more of the working group and the discriminating criterial which the social group consciously or intuitively prefers'. At the same conference, the director of personnel for Smith Industries suggested that companies first 'carry out job evaluation exercises in camera, or unilaterally'– as the *Irish Times* noted, implicitly excluding unions.[68]

With Ireland confronting growing levels of unemployment in 1975, calls were mounting not only to include inability-to-pay clauses in the proposed legislation, but also to defer its introduction as a whole. While the government announced that deferral would be allowed to the end of 1977 for private sector firms where equal pay would lead to loss of employment, the EEC rejected Ireland's request for a derogation, so equal pay for equal work became a legal entitlement from 1 January 1976.[69]

In January 1976 the *Irish Times*'s industrial correspondent Patrick Nolan laid the blame for the deferral squarely at the door of the trade union movement:

> The trade unions and the Irish Congress of Trade Unions should examine their consciences about equal pay. If they do this honestly they will be compelled to admit they are largely responsible for the fact that it is not being implemented on time. In the private sector it was not a priority over the past three years. If it had been the legislative target – full application from 1 January 1976 – could have generally been met.

Nor did Nolan spare Matt Merrigan and the ATGWU:

> Even some left-wing trade unionists seem to have accepted a more gradual introduction of equal pay than envisaged by the Act. In March 1975, Mr Matt Merrigan announced that his union, the Amalgamated Transport and General Workers' Union, proposed it should be introduced in four instalments up to 1 January 1977 [...] True, he also said that the ATGWU intended to campaign more vigorously and if necessary to call strikes.[70]

Unions responded to the deferral with a petition and a mass meeting in Dublin's Mansion House on 15 January 1976. In remarks delivered on his behalf, Donal Nevin – former ICTU research officer, and subsequently to become Congress general secretary, who was pursing the matter in Brussels – told the meeting that the trade union movement as a whole could

68   *Irish Times*, 6 March 1975.
69   Ayres, op cit.
70   *Irish Times*, 8 January 1976.

not be exempted from criticism for its failure to pursue implementation of equal pay more vigorously, but noted that it had pressed strongly for the Equal Pay Act and would not stand over its deferment.[71]

With legislation deferred, 1976 saw the ATGWU refocus on pursuing equal pay at the workplace and sectoral level, scoring some important victories. It is notable that these victories were achieved despite the worsening economic situation and employers' dire warnings of the consequences of increasing women's pay.

In September, around 2,000 women employed in the sugar confectionary industry received the first instalments of equal pay agreements which provided for phased increases over 18 months or two years until they reached the level of their male colleagues. The equal pay increases totalled around £9 in aggregate and the companies concerned included Urney, Fry-Cadbury, Trebor, Lemon & Co, and Tayto. Equal pay had been secured in Rowntree-Mackintosh the previous year.

Commenting on the agreements, Matt Merrigan said that job evaluation had not been used and that the negotiations had been on a company-by-company basis. He also noted that the union had secured equal pay without phasing for women operative members in Ecco in Dundalk, Waterford Glass and Kosangas; for clerical members in builders' providers companies Brooks, Thomas and Heiton McFerron; and for women operatives in meat processors Anglo-Irish Meats (Dundalk) and Tunney Meats (Clones).[72]

Conclusion

Reflecting on the struggle for equal pay in his memoirs, Matt Merrigan wrote:

> When moves were made to introduce equal pay and equal access to all jobs the men put up token resistance but were overwhelmed by the tide of equality running strongly and the need to conform to the new legislation on equality and anti-discrimination. For once in the union vote, the women used their numerical superiority. Unions in such mixed situations, depending on the relative strength of the sexes, had to walk on eggs to retain organisational integrity in face of the contending claims which were mutually exclusive.[73]

While Merrigan's personal commitment to equal pay – and to gender equality more generally – was not in doubt, neither the ATGWU nor the

---

71 *Irish Times*, 16 January 1976.
72 *Irish Times*, 8 September 1976.
73 Merrigan, *Eggs and Rashers*.

wider trade union movement appear to have had a worked out long-term strategy to eliminate gender pay differentials. Notwithstanding the 'numerical superiority' in certain workplaces or sectors which Merrigan referred to, women's concerns were incidental rather than central to unions' bargaining agendas – the subject of special women's conferences, such as the 1975 ATGWU women's conference, or the ICTU women's 'advisory committee' which produced a Women's Charter in August 1976. Nor did women have a seat at the negotiating table: in 1975, women's rights campaigner Nuala Fennell pointed out that, out of 300 full-time union personnel (referring, presumably, to officers rather than staff) in the Republic, just eight were female.[74] As late as 1979, the *Irish Times* noted that there were no women on the executives of the ICTU or the executives of the two largest unions, the ITGWU and the Federated Workers Union of Ireland (FWUI), and only one woman on the 24-person executive of the ATGWU.[75]

Although the ATGWU failed to follow through on the ambitious programme of demands backed up by strike action announced at the union's women's conference in 1975, it scored significant successes in individual workplaces and sectors between 1969 and 1976.

The struggle for equality continued, as did attempts by conservative forces – whether in government or in boardrooms – to use economic circumstances as a reason to halt or reverse progress. Speaking at an ICTU women's seminar in November 1984, Matt Merrigan – then president of Congress – noted that employers were using the recession to depress women's pay and use more of them in a casual capacity: 'It has been demonstrated clearly now and in the past that employers, and governments which have an employer orientation, in periods of mass unemployment and economic recession try to roll back the gains and power positions achieved by working people in more congenial times'.[76]

Alex Klemm is Unite Press and Media Coordinator for the Republic of Ireland.

74　Letter to the Editor, *Irish Times*, 5 March 1976.
75　*Irish Times*, 21 September 1979.
76　*Irish Times*, 19 November 1984.

8

Victory and Issues of Trade Union Power

Bathgate, Scotland: Working-class Morale Restored

The Scottish county of West Lothian sits midway between Edinburgh and Glasgow. By the early 1960s it had lost almost all of its coal mines and most heavy industry and had levels of unemployment significantly higher than the Scottish average – itself almost double that for the English Midlands. By 1960 just one pit remained in operation at Polkemmet and two iron foundries, one at Whitburn and the other at Armadale, both operated by North British Steel. Wages were low – over a third lower than comparable wage rates in England's industrial heartland. The area was visibly derelict: scarred by disused railway lines, old pit bings and the even bigger spoil tips left by shale oil mining that ended in the 1920s.

This was the area chosen in 1960 for what was to become the first of the BMC's new branch plants in the north and west. The factory opened in 1961 with 5,000 workers just outside Bathgate and adjacent to the main Glasgow–Edinburgh road. It produced buses, trucks and ultimately tractors. Components were driven up by lorry from Longbridge and other Midlands factories. For the BMC management Bathgate was seen as a problem factory – largely because of the long supply route, still over unimproved roads that sometimes became impassable in winter, and a new workforce drawn from a variety of backgrounds. There was a high labour turnover and there was also a relatively large number of unofficial stoppages and strikes. Over the first five years these were mainly over working conditions and health and safety – only one on pay. But the plant's low pay was also what made it a paying proposition for BMC.

By 1965, however, an effective JSSC had been established – representing 70 AEU stewards, 33 from the NUVB and 25 from the TGWU and small numbers from clerical grades, draughtsmen and the ETU. It was then that Jim Swan, a future chair of the JSSC, joined the workforce. He had previously worked as an engineer in the merchant marine and then at a foundry in Wishaw 15 miles from his home in Whitburn. He moved to

BMC because it was closer and the wages were slightly better. He was soon active with the AEU branch and by the early 1970s also a shop steward.[1]

Jim remembers the growing effectiveness and authority of the JSSC in the later 1960s.

> Links with the national combine committee were important and we got a lot of support from Dick Etheridge at Longbridge. We were joined by skilled workers from Glasgow, looking for better housing during the house demolitions of the late 60s and early 70s. They came from the Rolls Royce, Singers and the shipyards and brought with them a lot of union experience. The ex-miners were also important from that angle – although they always wanted to get back to the pits and missed the camaraderie there.[2]

By the late 1960s the high and growing level of inflation brought wages centre stage and an increasing number of stoppages occurred, though the differential with the Midlands remained. Solidarity actions also became increasingly important. In the summer of 1971 the plant voted to take strike action in support of the UCS workers. Jim remembers the banner specially painted for the monster demonstration in Glasgow in August 1971 – the biggest since 1919 – and the weekly levy on wages contributed from Bathgate to support the work-in. After 20 years of closures in West Lothian's old industries, the 'right to work' had a special resonance. Six months later came the miners' strike. Workers in Bathgate mobilised support for the one remaining local pit at Polkemmet where quite a number of its employees had previously worked. Any movement of coal into the Bathgate plant was stopped. The miners' victory, and 27 per cent pay rise, then helped provide the impetus for the strike at BMC Bathgate which began in February 1972, lasted seven weeks and finally secured approximate wage parity with the Midlands.

Jim remembers being out on picket duty in the snow that February. Only a few pickets were required as lorries immediately stopped and turned back. The drivers were almost all unionised by the TGWU. It was a long strike, seven weeks – with top management determined to maintain the differential. There were moments of crisis when pressure was brought to bear on workers – fearful of losing their jobs at a time of high and rising unemployment. Yet the strike held firm and eventually the management capitulated.

---

1 Jim Swan, interview by John Foster, 25 May 2020, United Oral History Archive. Other material comes from Catriona MacDonald, 'The Shopfloor Experience of Regional Policy 1961–1986', PhD thesis (Glasgow University, 2013).

2 Jim Swan, interview by John Foster, 25 May 2020.

The victory marked the final end of the differential after almost ten years and was the last of a series of strikes that had rumbled through the BMC/BL's regional plants which had been merged into one giant company in 1968.[3] It resulted in a plateau of worker confidence in Bathgate and elsewhere that was to continue through to the later 1970s. Jim Swan recalls that up to that point there had been a culture of bullying in the plant. This now ended. Big advances were made on health and safety – especially after the 1974 Labour Government Act that gave workers legal powers to halt work – and the BL combine itself was brought into state ownership. Even in West Lothian, battered by two generations of de-industrialisation, the tide of worker confidence and optimism had returned by the spring of 1972.

Preparing for Battle: TGWU Region 6 Merseyside and the North West

Further south in the TGWU's new Region 6, Merseyside's long-standing traditions of working-class solidarity were continuing to transform political horizons. Region 6 had been created at the instigation of Jack Jones through the merger of the previous Merseyside and Manchester/North West regions. The first meeting was held on 3 February 1970 at the TGWU headquarters, 1 The Crescent, Salford.[4]

This heard a resolution from the Merseyside Building and Construction Trades District Committee calling for George Brown to be stripped of his union sponsorship on account of his support for the Vietnam war. The second meeting on 5 May 1970 elected delegates to the British Campaign for Peace in Vietnam, sent a delegation to Romania and passed a resolution, despite opposition, condemning the US invasion of Cambodia. The meeting also voted to advertise in the *Morning Star for* May Day, condemned the exclusion of non-Labour Party delegates to the Swinton and Pendlebury Trades Council and voted to support the dockers coordinating committee's token strike in favour of docks nationalisation.

Following the Conservative election victory, the November meeting agreed total opposition to the Industrial Relations Bill and expressed concern at the growth in unemployment. It approved payments of £136,000 to support the Liverpool docks dispute. The next meeting on 2 February 1971 approved the ordering of special trains to take demonstrators to the 21 February demonstration in London. The 3 August meeting – on a motion from the Liverpool and Birkenhead docks – called for a reconsideration of all productivity deals in light of the further rise in unemployment

3 Murden, 'Demands for Fair Wages'.
4 MRC MSS 126/TG/102/1/1, Region 6 minutes 1970–1978.

to over 5 per cent. The meeting also noted that, despite the unemployment, union membership in the region had risen by 1,500. Note was taken both of the 'sweeping gains made by the Labour Party in the local elections' and of 'the considerable number of small demonstrations being organised throughout the region' against the new Industrial Relations Act and voted for resources to go into the 'mass demonstration being organised by the Labour Party and TUC'.[5]

The November 1971 meeting backed a motion from the Merseyside Building and Construction District Committee to agree a further donation to the UCS appeal and noted the funds already sent and 'still being taken at all levels'. The region deprecated 'actions taken by some union sponsored MPs in voting against the policies of the union' and in support of the Common Market. It welcomed the vote moved by Jack Jones at the TUC opposing entry and the motion from Harry Urwin instructing all unions to refuse to register under the Industrial Relations Act. The May 1972 Committee greeted the victory of the miners and applauded the solidarity action of other trade unionists across the country, 'primarily the TGWU', and particularly the role of the 'TGWU drivers'. The meeting expressed grave concern at the Conservative government's Housing Finance Act and its implications for working-class rents. The regional secretary also reported on the 'interim orders' taken out against the union under the Industrial Relations Act as a result of the Liverpool docks dispute.[6]

This dispute appears to have been engineered by a minority of employers and probably by sections of the judiciary in collusion with some elements of the Cabinet. On Merseyside, as we have seen, the issues around containerisation had been resolved by an agreement between TGWU members in road haulage and the docks shop stewards that all work in the new container docks to the north of the city be handled by registered dockers. On 20 March 1972 a document drawn up to this effect by the docks shop stewards was signed by virtually all dock employers. One firm resisted: Heatons. This firm was then picketed and as a result appealed to the National Industrial Relations Court which imposed, at this stage, relatively modest fines on the TGWU. In April the TUC under the guidance of its general secretary, Vic Feather, and despite opposition from Jack Jones and Hugh Scanlon, changed its position on total boycott and agreed that, if challenged in the courts under the Act, fines should be paid.[7]

5 MRC MSS 126/TG/102/1/1, Minutes of Region 6 Committee, 3 August 1971.

6 MRC MSS 126/TG/102/1/1, Minutes of Region 6 Committee, 2 May 1972.

7 Fred Lindop, 'The Dockers and the 1971 Industrial Relations Act, Part 1: Shop Stewards and Containerization', HSIR, 1998, vol.5, no.1, pp.33–72.

The Dockers Victorious: Industrial Relations Act
Fatally Compromised

March–April 1972 had witnessed the full public completion of the Conservative government's U-turn on economic policy – a reversal tentatively initiated the previous summer. Massive amounts of money were pumped into the re-floating of the shipyards on the Upper Clyde. Regional policy was re-instated and subsidies restored for firms in depressed regions. As workplace occupations gathered pace in Scotland, Yorkshire, the North West and London, policies to combat unemployment suddenly became a government priority. At the same time, in April 1972, the government approached Vic Feather and the TUC for discussions on economic policy. On 3 May the TGWU paid the fines imposed for the picketing of Heatons by stewards acting, in legal terms, as 'servants' of the union. In May *The Times* declared a new outbreak of peace between the government and the TUC. Very shortly after that a joint committee was established chaired by Jack Jones for the TGWU and Lord Aldington, chair of the Port of London and friend of the prime minister, to work out an interim settlement to resolve the issue of the 'temporary unregistered reserve' of dockers.[8]

It would appear that the government's advisers – including some employers and senior Ministry of Employment civil servants – believed that divisions among TGWU members, particularly the dispute between dockers and commercial drivers in London, and between shop stewards and union officers in Liverpool and Hull, left the militant wing weakened. They seem to have hoped that, along with the new relations being developed with the TUC, a division could be engineered between Jack Jones and the TGWU's more militant members. This in turn appeared to offer the prospect of creating a division over tactics that would help isolate the LCDTU. At the beginning of June further fines, significantly higher, were imposed on the TGWU for the continued picketing of Heatons. Again the TGWU paid up.

The response of the LCDTU was to hold a conference on 10 June to consolidate its mandate. This was attended by 1,500 delegates representing 500 trade union branches, shop stewards committees and some union district committees. The conference agreed that should anyone be arrested under the terms of the Act there should be an immediate strike across all workplaces – a shot across the bows of the right wing in the TUC as well as the government.[9]

In response, the government and its advisers shifted the focus of their attack from Liverpool to London where there were clear divisions

---

8 Jack Jones, *Union Man*, p.255.

9 Much of this section and earlier sections is drawn from Seifert and Sibley, *Revolutionary Communist*.

within the TGWU membership over the ongoing dispute at the Chobham container depot. On 15/16 June Lord Donaldson, acting for the Industrial Relations Court, ordered the arrest of three shop stewards who had been picketing the Chobham depot to stop the movement of containers by (mainly) TGWU drivers' road haulage section. Immediately the London dockers came out en masse.

Unfortunately for the government the arrests coincided with a key moment in the final disintegration of the Bretton Woods agreement which had linked an overvalued dollar and an even more overvalued pound sterling to gold. With the Bank's gold reserves almost exhausted, a dock strike blocking exports was the last thing the government could afford. An immediate solution was sought. Examining the TGWU's submission to the Appeal Court, Lord Denning now found that the stewards had been acting as 'agents' and not 'servants' of the union and therefore were not bound by the terms of Act. They were immediately released. The following week, on 26 June, Vic Feather gained the agreement of a majority of the TUC General Council to offer a further compromise to the government. This was that the TUC would consider a limited acceptance of the Act and would argue at the September 1972 TUC Congress that it was not effective to use strike action to oppose the Act.

However, this was not the end of the story. The following week, the owners of the Midland dock in London (where the main shareholders were the Vesteys, the millionaire imported meat monopolists) initiated another legal attack on TGWU members who were picketing the dock. Using private detectives they accumulated evidence against five docker shop stewards that enabled them to be accused of 'organising' the pickets and hence being 'servants' and not agents. Lord Donaldson issued arrest warrants from the National Industrial Relations Court (NICR) on Friday 21 July – coinciding with the beginning of the holiday period. The dock employers asked the government to declare a state of emergency. By Saturday all five dockers had been arrested and placed in Pentonville prison. The government and its advisers seemed to have hoped that the onset of the holidays and inaction by the TUC would carry them through.

The leaders of the LCDTU ensured this did not happen. The dockers came out immediately and were followed by the London printers. A mass meeting of print workers had been organised for the Saturday to support the continuing work-in at Briant Colour. The chair of the LCDTU Kevin Halpin addressed it – winning support of the leaderships of SOGAT and NATSOPA and the Fleet Street electricians. The entire meeting marched off to Pentonville prison. No Sunday papers appeared the following morning and most did not reappear till late the following week. On the Sunday Halpin addressed a mass meeting of train drivers at Waterloo. On Monday trains were stopped. First thing on Monday morning Halpin along with Eric Rechnitz addressed a mass dockside meeting of haulage drivers, previously in conflict with the dockers, and won their support.

After that he travelled to Glasgow at the invitation of Ray MacDonald, TGWU regional secretary, to ensure Scotland came out. Through Monday telephone messages came in from workplace after workplace. All were either already out on strike or would be out the following day, 25 July.[10] On Wednesday, under the pressure of this mass movement, the TUC General Council then itself called a General Strike, the first since 1926. By then, however, on 26 July, government lawyers had found another legal technicality and the stewards were released.

A veteran of docks, Jack Dash wrote the following month:

> The impact of the arrest was immediate: a wind of fury rose up to a storm of anger and brought about a spontaneity of united action from all trades and professions never experienced in the post-war years, so fierce that the Knights of the TUC Round Table were forced to stop shadow boxing and reluctantly threaten a 24-hour general strike unless the men were released. But the Pentonville Five did not have to spend another weekend away from their families. The grass roots rank and file had forced the government to release the five, and the most tremendous victory of the post-war industrial struggles was achieved.[11]

Across Britain, the docks and much of the transport, all large engineering works, print and the coal industry were paralysed for at least three days and in some cases more.

The print workers were the first to move. Stopping the Sunday papers sent an immediate signal across Britain. One NATSOPA member, later Father of the Night Machine Chapel at the *Daily Express*, Brian Porter, remembers it well.[12] He was quite young at the time, a trade union member but not yet much involved. He had not been at the Briant Colour meeting but that afternoon, going into work to print the *News of the World*, he heard the Day Chapel at the *Express* had voted for strike action. Along with others he contacted Bill Harding, Father of Night Chapel, for a meeting. The print workers were unanimous: no return till the dockers were released. They left immediately – shutting down the biggest circulation Sunday paper. On the Monday he remembers the march to Pentonville prison starting from Tower Hill. When it reached Pentonville Road he was amazed at the numbers. Everything was at a standstill. All the roads were blocked. There was a bus immobilised. The marchers started to rock it. The dockers' stewards intervened: 'there are

---

10 Halpin, *Memoirs*, pp.120–121.

11 Quoted by Seifert and Sibley, *Revolutionary Communist*, p.185 from Jack Dash in *Labour Monthly*, September 1972.

12 The Father of the Night Chapel was responsible for convening shop stewards during the night shift during which newspapers were printed.

people on that bus' and then escorted the passengers off along with the driver and conductor.[13]

It was the Monday that saw the biggest battles in workplaces on whether or not to join what was still an unofficial strike. Some of the most difficult were in the East End itself where conflicts between dockers, drivers and ship repair workers had been common. Among the ship repair workers George Anthony helped lead the push for solidarity. He was then AEU convener at the Albert Dock's Tyne and Wear repair yard. His first attempt in the morning was disrupted by a right-wing chargehand. He called another meeting at midday. Meantime he contacted the dockers to send women to the gates. By the time of the meeting female staff from the Greater London Authority (GLA) canteen were handing out leaflets. The objection went up – 'the dockers are pinching our work'. He replied: 'that doesn't justify prison'. Eventually the meeting voted unanimously to come out: 'no return till the dockers are released'. That Wednesday he was at the great demonstration at Pentonville along with Dennis Skinner and Bill Freeman when there was a push to try to take the prison. He intervened – seeing from his vantage point the masses of police concealed behind the wall: 'go back to your workplaces. The TUC, Jack Jones and Hughie Scanlon have now officially called a general strike. Ensure every single remaining worker comes out'. That very afternoon the government's own amicus curiae, the Official Solicitor, who was watching the demonstration, got the dockers released.[14]

Elsewhere in London, and across Britain, the response had been massive – despite the summer holidays. Frank Cooper, member of the District Committee of the Sheetmetal Workers and Convener of Willards Ventilation in Battersea, was present at the Saturday demonstration with the Sheetmetal Workers banner. 'There were banners from every union and a great spirit of comradeship and solidarity'. On the Monday Frank moved the vote for stoppage back in Battersea. It was unanimous – boiler-makers and engineers, sheet metal workers and TGWU members all voted to come out till the dockers were released.

In the docks themselves the response was immediate. Brian Holmes and Kevin Hussey had both been picketing Chobham Farm and the Vestey's Union Cold Store the previous week, the former a TGWU member, and a member of Vic Turner's branch, and the second a stevedore. As soon as they heard of the arrests, work was halted across the docks.

People congregated at Tower Hill, the traditional meeting place. Thousands and thousands. Printers. Engineers. Some said go to

---

13 Brian Porter, interview by John Foster, February 2021, United Oral History Archive.

14 George Anthony, interview by John Foster, February 2021, United Oral History Archive.

Figure 6: Vic Turner carried from Pentonville Jail 1972
(Unite Photo Archive)

Parliament. We said march to the prison. The police were brushed aside. As they walked, people joined from all walks of life. All trades. Housewives. Construction workers walked off the building sites. It was the movement that was determined to win. Us dockers could never have done it on our own.[15]

It was Brian Holmes who, along with his father-in-law, Jack Malloy, carried Vic Turner, their branch Chairman, out from the jail – demonstrating the strength of the docklands' closely-knit communities but also the end-result of nationwide solidarity.

The following day, 27 July, dockers, celebrating their victory, assembled outside Transport House to hear the outcome of the dockers' delegate vote on whether to accept the agreement drawn up by Lord Aldington and Jack Jones from the committee established earlier in

15 Brian Holmes and Kevin Hussey, interview by John Foster, February 2021, Unite Oral History Archive.

the summer. They were in triumphant mood. The deal made some provision for guaranteed jobs as well as redundancy payments, but did not guarantee continued employment for all. The dockers' delegates rejected the deal. The leaders of the unofficial dockers' shop stewards committee, including the recently released Bernie Steer and Vic Turner, led the opposition and won the call for a national strike to secure full guarantees. *The Times* described the scene:

> When the decision was announced the square became a sea of bobbing banners and placards [...]. Several shop stewards were carried shoulder high [...] dockers kissed and hugged each other. Special cheers were reserved for Mr Vic Turner and Mr Cornelius Clancy, two of those who had spent five days in prison.[16]

The Jones-Aldington Committee then went into intensive discussions. *The Times* for 12 August reported that the government was placing pressure on the employers to make concessions and on 17 August a meeting of dock delegates voted to accept the new offer and end the strike. The shop stewards liaison committee attempted to continue an unofficial strike but only managed to win dockside votes in Liverpool and Manchester. The new provisions guaranteed employment for all existing dockers, including those not currently registered, as well as making more generous provision available for those who wished to leave the industry.

For the dockers it was not a complete victory. The process of containerisation went on and the docks were not nationalised. But they had forced the government to guarantee all existing dockers employment and, in the course of doing so, inflicted mortal damage on the Industrial Relations Act itself. From that moment it lived only a twilight existence and was never again used to imprison trade unionists. No less important, the strike established the authority of the LCDTU and restored the tactic of the political general strike to the armoury of the trade union movement after half a century.

At the subsequent Cabinet meeting, on 1 August, Edward Heath presented a paper on civil emergencies. This created yet another special emergency committee. This one was to be chaired by the prime minister or his deputy to oversee all future crises (another Cabinet paper from the same meeting is still listed in the National Archives as 'withdrawn from circulation'). Also meeting that day was the TGWU Region 6 Committee in the North West. This approved motions 'for transmission to GEC' calling for immediate solidarity action on behalf of any members penalised as a result of the strikes. It also noted, in light of the decision of the TUC General Council, a motion from Chisholm district calling for immediate

16 *The Times*, 28 July 1972.

industrial action should any trade unionist be jailed and for the TUC to call a one-day General Strike. After 'long discussion' it was additionally agreed that the General Council of the TUC was the only body that could call a General Strike.[17]

A New Turning Point?

This moment in July 1972 was a historic one, both in terms of the political evolution of the TGWU and of the British labour movement. In 1926 the TGWU had played a key role in mobilising for the 1926 General Strike, but had then allowed itself to be deceived by the government (and the trade union right wing) into abandoning it. Subsequently Ernest Bevin had been corralled by the government and major employers into justifying this abandonment and, within 18 months, into leading the TUC into discussions with the big monopolies which resulted in the public abandonment of any immediate socialist objectives in favour of a policies of gradual amelioration.

This in turn shifted the political balance within the Labour Party to the right. It resulted in half a century in which there developed an almost unbridgeable rift between those within the working-class movement who argued for the necessity of challenging capitalist state power and those saw the role of the trade union movement and the Labour Party as that of gradual amelioration. These years saw the expulsion of communists and their left-wing allies from the Labour Party in the later 1920s, the break with the Independent Labour Party in 1929–1931 and by the 1940s the TGWU's deep involvement in the international politics of the Cold War, with communists and supporters banned from any office in the union. It also saw a concentration of power in the hands of the TGWU's appointed officers and an intermittent civil war with shop stewards and rank-and-file organisations. As we have seen, it was Frank Cousins who reversed these policies, challenged the right wing in the Labour Party and actively encouraged shop steward democracy.

Jack Jones continued this work. Summer 1972 witnessed the dramatic results. For the following decade political one-day general strikes became part of the armoury of the trade union movement. The Left consolidated a position of leadership. The Labour Party once more talked about transforming the balance of class power: its 1973 pre-election policy document called for 'an irreversible shift of wealth and power in favour of working people',[18] a position carried forward into the two general elections of 1974.

17 MRC MSS 126/TG/102/1/1, Region 6 minutes, 1 August 1972.
18 Labour Party Manifesto, 1974.

To this extent 1972 did mark a historic turning point. A mobilised working class continued to demonstrate its power, rallying to defend the workers at ConMech and then the miners in February 1974. The spate of workplace occupations, well over a hundred, spread across the country in 1972–1973, evidenced both a willingness of workers to risk their own immediate interests to defend the principle of the right to work and the wider support forthcoming from surrounding working-class communities.[19] So did the actions of trade unionists in support of local councils and tenants risking imprisonment for defying the Tory's Housing Finance Act of 1972. As we noted previously, the 1973 biennial conference completed this policy reversal with demands that the next Labour government embark on extensive nationalisation, end any wage control legislation and repeal all anti-trade union laws. It also demonstrated an understanding of the need for the trade union movement to maintain continued mobilisation on the ground with its motion on action committees to oppose closures and support actions on rents and other social issues.

This was a far cry from the pacified, non-political and consumerist working class claimed by Abrams, Hilden and Rose to exist in 1959 – or even the 'instrumental', pay hungry but 'non-solidaristic' car workers described by John Goldthorpe for the early 1960s.[20] It was, however, not a development that occurred automatically or which was somehow directed from above. As we have seen, it resulted from thousands of localised battles in which workers challenged managements, learned lessons and developed confidence. No less, it was also a political process. People argued and discussed. Attitudes and cultures changed – and relatively central to that was the position of the organised Left, centred on the Communist Party but including many others. In all the major factories, rail depots and pits, dozens and sometimes hundreds of copies of the *Morning Star* were bought daily. The readers formed the core of the new shop stewards movement that emerged in the 1960s, providing the local activists for the LCDTU who took their politics into the district and regional committees of the TGWU, AEU, TASS, SOGAT, NATSOPA and the National Union of Mineworkers (NUM). Without this combined activity there would have been no General Strike on 24–27 July.[21]

As remembered by Gary Fabian, then a leading steward at Rolls Royce Corniche in West London, 'its success was greatly assisted' by the prior development of the network of shop stewards committees and what were called combines, or national combine committees' with an initial history 'in the aircraft industry and [which] were originally called allied trade shop

19 Mills, 'Worker Occupations 1971–1975'.
20 M. Abrams, R. Hinden and R. Rose, *Must Labour Lose?* (Penguin, 1959); J. Goldthorpe, D. Lockwood, F. Bechofer and J. Platt, *Affluent Worker* (Cambridge University Press, 1969).
21 Seifert and Sibley, *Revolutionary Communist*, pp.182–185.

stewards national councils and were thought to be largely influenced by the Communist Party. [...] Combines sprung up in the motor industry, there was a Rolls Royce combine, a Vickers combine, a British Leyland combine and a British Aerospace combine.[22]

This was, moreover, a movement of actual people, arguing, thinking, organising for themselves and not directed by Jack Jones or, for that matter, by the liaison committee. People worked out plans of action for themselves, locally, collectively, in their own immediate circumstances even though there was – through the shop stewards movement and union-wide 'Lefts' – a degree of central coordination. Coordinated action, when it occurred – as on 24–27 July – had to be argued for in specific circumstances as Kevin Halpin himself understood and demonstrated. This understanding is also important too for the next stage of the story.

Jack Jones, Edward Heath and the Origins of the Social Contract

In 1972 something of a divergence began to emerge between Jack Jones and the political positions taken by sections of the shop stewards movement, the LCDTU and the Communist Party. In 1972 these differences were only tactical and on most things there was a general unity of perspective. But by 1974–1977 this was not the case. Jack Jones had become one of the architects of the Labour government's social contract and in consequence became a supporter of its incomes policy. In this he found himself posed against others resisting it. This conflict will be discussed in the next volume. But because the origins to go back to our current period it is important that it is also discussed here.

Summer–Autumn 1972 was when the policy document, *Economic Policy and the Cost of Living*,[23] was drafted by the Joint TUC Labour Party Liaison Committee established earlier in the year largely on the initiative of Jack Jones. The document itself was published in November 1972 but elements of it were incorporated in the motion moved by Jack Jones at the September 1972 TUC conference. This outlined how and when an incomes policy might be accepted – in terms largely directed against the current Heath government: 'No consideration can be given to any policy on incomes unless it is an integral part of an economic strategy which includes control of rents, profits, dividends, prices and is designed to secure a redistribution of income nationally and globally'.[24]

22 Gary Fabian, then a shop steward at Rolls Royce Corniche in West London, written statement, February 2021, held in the Unite Virtual Archive.
23 TUC Labour Party Liaison Committee, *Economic Policy and the Cost of Living* (TUC, 1972).
24 *The Times*, September 1972; Jones, *Union Man*, p.238.

The motion went on to call for price controls, particularly on food prices, the withdrawal of the Housing Finance Act and controls over property and land speculation. Jones ended quoting Ernest Bevin: 'you cannot place a ceiling on wages when one man works for another man's profit'.[25] All this was fully supported across the Left in 1972.

However, when Labour took office in 1974 on a radical programme calling for 'an irreversible shift in the balance of wealth and power', the question was immediately posed. Did this commitment warrant and require trade unionists to agree to an incomes policy? The Labour government did have a radical programme. Not all of it was implemented. But significant sections were – in terms of widespread public ownership, a repeal of anti-trade union laws and health and safety legislation that pushed back on the prerogatives of management. Was this enough to justify ending wage struggle in a period of very high inflation, ultimately producing a significant decline in real wages by 1977?

The argument of the Left was that the Wilson government had not transformed the nature of state power. Key economic decisions were still taken in response to the demands of the Bank of England, the City and the IMF. Politically those in the Labour Party leadership who opposed the party's socialist direction remained entrenched and in 1975–1976 seized control. Correspondingly, pressure was exerted through the trade union movement itself to downgrade activity on wages, threatening to place shop stewards in conflict with those who they represented. Across the country, the motive force for any fundamental change, the trade union and labour movement, itself became divided.[26]

Nonetheless, the debate of 1973–1974 was a legitimate one and remains so. How does the organised working class, as represented by trade unions, politically consolidate its intermediate political gains within a system that remains ruled by the interests of capital – and in our period, very large-scale capital indeed? In what ways can trade union leaders strike deals with government?

This in 1972 was already a dilemma for Jack Jones and the TUC and underlay Jack Jones's wish to develop policy on how the trade union movement negotiated with government. Heath wanted to maintain what he saw as the tripartite balance between government, trade unions and business that underlay what he considered to be the post-war consensus in Britain, and wished to do so particularly as the country formally entered the European Community. By late 1971 and early 1972 Heath had largely isolated those on the far right of the Cabinet and moved to draw the TUC into tripartite discussions with the CBI and the government. The general

---

25 Jones, *Union Man*, p.238.
26 These dilemmas are discussed in detail in Seifert and Sibley, *Revolutionary Communist*, pp.216 ff.

secretary of the TUC Vic Feather wanted to respond positively. Feather was, as Jones noted, drawn to people of influence and power 'like a moth to a candle' and Feather was backed in his wish to respond by right-wingers in the General Council.[27] The question was whether Jack Jones (along with Hugh Scanlon) should themselves join it and seek to mitigate any adverse consequences – and seize any positive opportunities. Feather held out the prospect that Heath might drop the Industrial Relations Act in return for cooperation in other areas.

In the midst of this, in March 1972, Heath also sought Jones's support in seeking a resolution of the dockers dispute on containerisation. From this the Jones-Aldington working party emerged. As we have seen, its deliberations overlapped with the climax of the confrontation with the Industrial Relations Act in June–July and the outcome was announced virtually at the same moment that the imprisoned dockers were released. The dockers did not see Jones' proposals as a victory or as in any way reflecting the power demonstrated by mass strike action over the previous days. As reflected in his autobiography, Jones felt somewhat out of sympathy with this position. He was forced to go back into negotiation. Jones was even more disgruntled when the further proposals for a settlement were subject to angry barracking by the assembled dockers on 19 August, even though the proposals were accepted by the meeting of dock delegates.[28]

Over the same summer Jones had also agreed to take part in Heath's tripartite discussions. Along with Vic Feather, there were two right-wingers, Allen of the Distributive Workers and Cooper of the Municipal Workers, while Jones was backed up by Hugh Scanlon of the engineers. By the autumn Scanlon had been instructed by his executive to withdraw and did so. Jones continued. He wanted to use the tripartite discussions as a forum for pressing issues of low pay and justice for pensioners. He also saw all the dangers of Feather and his right-wing colleagues stitching up a deal with Heath. Heath's priority was to get a deal on 'voluntary' wage restraint. The CBI wanted this as well, but with altogether no concessions that might impact adversely on members.

On 6 November 1972 Heath finally abandoned the attempt to secure binding agreements.[29] Shortly afterwards, in his review of government policy, he noted the need to strengthen the authority of both the TUC and the CBI over their members, in terms of much improved central staffing and media, and to consider funding by which this could be done. Both organisations were currently too weak, he considered, to form the basis for a tripartite consensus that could bind and control

27 Murray, *T&G Story*, pp.157.
28 Jones, *Union Man*, pp.245–254.
29 Middlemas, *Power, Competition and the State: Threats*, pp.354–355.

their respective members.[30] At the TGWU's 1973 biennial conference Jones defended his decision to take part in the tripartite negotiations: 'The Union should not place itself in a position of not talking when our people expect it of us. You do not pay me to sit dumb. You pay me to speak, to act, to help, to advise and part of the process is to publicly to present our case'.[31]

In these talks in 1972–1973 Jones did not compromise his principles. But the position in 1974 was more complicated. A radical programme had been secured. In part at least it was being implemented. Should, in these circumstances, pay bargaining be restrained and the organisation of workers on the ground stood down? This is a question that will be considered in the next volume.

Heath's Final Defeat: 'Who Runs This Country?'

The final 15 months of the Conservative government saw Heath embattled, seeing opposition growing, as he put it, on both 'extremes of the political spectrum'.[32] He sought to continue discussions with both the CBI and the TUC, though separately, on pay and prices and did so as currency turbulence, war in the Middle East and ever increasing oil prices pushed inflation to record levels. It was to little effect. He continued to cling to the wreckage of the Industrial Relations Act, even when major employers saw it as an obstacle to industrial peace and themselves paid the fines imposed on the engineers from the Con-Mech dispute.[33]

The government's strategy increasingly appears to have been based on the belief that the key battle was that of public opinion and that its main task was therefore to isolate and stigmatise what it saw as the hard Left. One example was the Housing Finance Act. This sought to transform council house tenure by shifting the 'subsidy' from the house to a means-tested payment to the tenant. The trade union movement, particularly the TGWU, saw it as a direct attack on the post-war guarantee of affordable housing for all. Its implementation by local councils saw widespread defiance by Labour councils. But in June 1973 the government decided, despite the many councils in defiance of the act, to select just three for legal penalty. These were councils such as Clay Cross and Lambeth with leading left-wingers in charge and with close links to local working-class communities and tenants movements. It was here, as an example to the

30 TNA CAB 129/166/1, Heath, 'Review of Government Strategy', 17 November 1972 and CAB 129/167/1, 12 January 1973.
31 Jones, *Union Man*, p.259.
32 TNA CAB 129/164/24, Heath to Cabinet, September 1972.
33 Seifert and Sibley, *Revolutionary Communist*, p.186.

rest, that councillors were to be disqualified and surcharged and held up to public ridicule by the press.[34]

The same approach was also adopted in industrial relations. Summer 1972 had seen building workers across the country taking strike action to achieve basic minimum conditions of employment and pay as outlined in the Building Workers Charter. It was a rank-and-file movement that united workers across different trades and unions – including the TGWU – and gave workers in what was a casualised, dangerous and poorly paid industry an effective bargaining power for the first time. As with the miners' strike at the beginning of the year it used flying pickets very effectively to close down sites across the country. Eventually the workers won official union backing including that of the TGWU, and after five weeks of strike action, on 15 September, the employers made a settlement that gave building workers their biggest rise in the history of the industry.

The government did not act against the unions involved. But it did against the leaders of the Building Workers Charter – and significantly perhaps – it initiated the action in November 1972 after the breakdown of the tripartite talks. Chief constables were instructed to collect evidence that would enable the prosecution of the leaders. This would not to be under the Industrial Relations Act but under the 1875 Conspiracy Act. Arrests began in February–March 1973 and the trial took place with considerable publicity in Shrewsbury in July 1973. As with the Clay Cross prosecutions, the government, it appears, saw it as essentially an ideological operation to shift public opinion against what it wanted to portray as the violent and anti-constitutional Left. It made significant preparations to do so. The government's specialist anti-communist Information Research Department worked with the BBC, as it had during the ETU trial, to produce a TV programme hosted by Woodrow Wyatt entitled *The Red under the Bed*. This was shown during the trial itself. Three leaders, one a well-known communist, Des Warren, were given heavy prison sentences of up to three years. Eventually, after long years of campaigning, the convictions were overturned by the Court of Appeal in March 2021 after it was revealed that all the police statements, at the time denied to the defence, had already been destroyed by, or before, the original trial. The actual conspiracy, on the evidence now available, was clearly by the government and not those put in prison.[35]

Four months later the same approach underlay the government's approach to the miners' claim for a wage settlement that would bring

34 TNA CAB 129/170/11 and 20 Rippon, Housing Finance Act, 19 June 1973 and 16 July 1973.
35 Jim Arnison, *The Shrewsbury Three* (Lawrence and Wishart, 1974); Seifert and Sibley, *Revolutionary Communist*; Diarmid Kelleher, 'The Spatial Politics of Violence: The Picket Line in 1970s Britain', *Transactions Institute of British Geographers*, April 2020; *The Times* 24 March 2021.

them into line with the gains made by other workers. The new employment secretary Maurice Macmillan outlined government tactics in a long memorandum to the Cabinet on 27 November 1973. It was to orchestrate a public relations campaign that would 'build up the weight of popular opinion hostile to the militants to the point where the NUM moderates could win the day'.[36] It suggested using the usual channels and, on this occasion, even drawing on the Conservative Party's organisation in constituencies to produce and circulate leaflets. Such a public relations campaign, bringing maximum pressure to bear on the NUM moderates, and isolating the Lefts such as McGahey and Scargill, was, for Macmillan, the only way to go. Forcing a ballot among NUM members was dangerous as it would probably produce the wrong result – and using the Industrial Relations Act equally so. But conceding the claim would be 'pure capitulation'. For the following two months the government's entire attention was focused on winning this battle, on how to secure additional supplies of oil, consulting with industry on how to conserve energy supplies and how, legally, to cut off any support through social security for the families of striking miners (a task given to the right-wing ideologue Keith Joseph).[37]

When the NUM nonetheless went ahead and did so with the support of the TUC, and critically the TGWU, the government called an election. In its election broadcasts government speakers posed the issue as being about who should rule Britain. Was it the elected government or the militants on the Left? The Communist Party's industrial organiser Bert Ramelson was specifically named in the election broadcasts.[38] Despite a massive propaganda campaign, the government lost.

What, then, is the balance sheet for the TGWU in this final phase of the battle against the government's anti-trade union offensive?

Jack Jones himself trod a careful path, both maintaining relations with the government and holding the right wing in check within the TUC. He supported continuing talks with the government while Scanlon, the engineers, the draughtsmen and a number of other 'Left' unions opposed. But he also ensured that the TGWU backed the engineers and the Left in demanding complete non-cooperation with the Industrial Relations Act. Additionally and very astutely Jones also consolidated the ground for the biggest gain of 1972: the use of the general strike weapon for political purposes. At the 1973 TUC he successfully moved a resolution that committed the TUC to secure

36 TNA CAB 129/173/3, Maurice Macmillan, 'Handling of the Miners and Power Engineers disputes', 27 November 1973. Heath stressed the importance of moulding public opinion in 'Reorganisation of Responsibilities for Improving the Projection of Government Policies', CAB 129/173/17 20 December 1973; Middlemas, *Power, Competition and the State: Threats*, p.378.

37 TNA CAB 129/174/7, Keith Joseph, 'Supplementary Benefit for Strikers' Families', 29 January 1974.

38 Seifert and Sibley, *Revolutionary Communist*, pp.206–208.

justice for pensioners and, when appropriate, to use the strike action to do so. 'To be old in Britain is to be poor. The scandal of this poverty must be wiped out. We can delay no longer'. It was the responsibility of the TUC to use its industrial power to secure justice. No one opposed.[39]

At the same Congress Harry Urwin, deputy general secretary, seconded Hugh Scanlon's motion – which was narrowly defeated – to commit the TUC to total non-cooperation, including the non-payment of fines, with the Industrial Relations Act and Court:

> The Act would only be defeated if the whole movement worked together under the leadership of Congress [...] A movement which cannot endure some sacrifice and maintain some discipline in its ranks when it is under attack like this soon ceases to be an effective movement at all.[40]

Jones himself intervened to put the case for continuing discussions with the government. 'Unions must be free to represent their members. Restrictions and constraints on their efforts are characteristic of a fascist society and intolerable to a free trade union movement. We favour the use of conciliation and voluntary impartial arbitration. We have tried to press that counsel on the government. They have virtually destroyed trust'. But he went on that the union case 'must be continued to be put the government' and that the movement 'needed to ensure the election of the Labour government that was committed beforehand to essential principles. The lie that wages caused inflation had been exploded'.[41] Jones's presence at the discussions ensured that Feather and the right wing did not concede basic principles, and, as far as it was possible, that the discussions did not play to Heath's attempt to isolate and defeat the 'militant' Left.

Yet it was the union's membership that actually made the history, the 'great tradition of independent working-class power', which Frank Cousins had argued for 14 years earlier. As Gary Fabian put it, it was 'the combination of rank and file marches and rallies [which] meant the TUC had to take notice'. None of this was automatic. It had to be argued for and won. 'On hearing the latest request to attend a march from the Liaison Committee [LCTU]' the response was 'to discuss it at works committee level and decide what action we would take and how many shop stewards we would send [...] what was noticeable was at each rally or demonstration the growing numbers of those attending'.[42]

39 *The Times*, 5 September 1973.
40 *The Times*, 4 September 1973.
41 *The Times*, 6 September 1973.
42 Gary Fabian, written statement in February 2021 of his memories of shop stewards responses at the Rolls Royce Corniche works (London): document held in the Unite virtual archive, 128 Theobald Road, London WC1X 8TN, contact Jim Mowatt.

The election result was in fact very close. Labour was just four seats ahead of the Conservatives. However, it remained a victory and was even more so given the ideological ground on which Heath had sought to fight it. Voters did not reject a socialism that was far harder-edged that anything seen for a generation and a manifesto that talked about an irreversible shift of wealth and power in favour of working people. It fittingly concludes a story that began with Frank Cousins challenging the Cold War politics of the Labour Party under Hugh Gaitskell. The ground had now shifted. And it was a trade union, the TGWU – now led by members not officials – that had, together with allied unions, changed the face of British politics.

Some Issues for Discussion

1. When Jack Jones said in 1973 that the trade union movement 'needed to ensure the election of the Labour government that was committed beforehand to essential principles' (*The Times*, 6 September 1973.), why did he say it, how far was this feasible and what steps might have been taken by the trade union movement to ensure a Labour government did deliver?

2. How far did Jack Jones's part in developing the 1972 Labour programme, *Economic Policy and the Cost of Living*, later limit his freedom and that of the TGWU under a Labour government?

3. 1972–1974 saw the trade union movement display a remarkable ability to mobilise solidarity action. What lessons can be learned?

4. How far was solidarity with, and practical support for, those struggling overseas against external domination or internal tyranny important for trade union activity in Britain and Ireland?

Index

Page numbers in **bold** refer to figures.